Serie: Bible Commentary of Ellen G White Writtings

1

THE SEVENTH DAY ADVENTIST BIBLE COMMENTARY VOLUME 1

Original Edition

Ellen G. White

Copyright ©2023
LS COMPANY
ISBN: 979-8-8689-7566-0

Content

Genesis 7

Chapter 1 7

Chapter 2 7

Chapter 3 9

Chapter 4 17

Chapter 5 19

Chapter 6 21

Chapter 7 26

Chapter 8 26

Chapter 9 27

Chapter 11 28

Chapter 12 29

Chapter 13 30

Chapter 14 30

Chapter 15 31

Chapter 18 32

Chapter 19 32

Chapter 22 33

Chapter 25 34

Chapter 28 35

Chapter 31 36

Chapter 32 36

Chapter 35 37

Chapter 37 37

Chapter 39 39

Chapter 41 41

Chapter 42 41

Chapter 45 41

Chapter 49 42

Exodus 43

Chapter 1 43

Chapter 2 43

Chapter 3 44

Chapter 4 45

Chapter 7 47

Chapter 8 47

Chapter 9 48

Chapter 11 48

Chapter 12 48

Chapter 14 49

Chapter 15 50

Chapter 16 50

Chapter 17 52

Chapter 18 53

Chapter 19 53

Chapter 20 54

Chapter 21 59

Chapter 23 60

Chapter 24...61
Chapter 25...62
Chapter 26...62
Chapter 27...62
Chapter 31...63
Chapter 32...65
Chapter 34...66
Leviticus...68
Chapter 1...68
Chapter 5...68
Chapter 8...69
Chapter 10...69
Chapter 14...70
Chapter 16...71
Chapter 17...71
Chapter 25...72
Numbers 74
Chapter 11...74
Chapter 12...74
Chapter 13...75
Chapter 14...76
Chapter 15...76
Chapter 16...77
Chapter 17...79
Chapter 20...80
Chapter 21...81

Chapter 22 81
Chapter 24 82
Chapter 25 83
Chapter 26 83
Chapter 29 83
Deuteronomy 84
Chapter 1 84
Chapter 4 85
Chapter 6 85
Chapter 9 86
Chapter 15 86
Chapter 18 87
Chapter 23 88
Chapter 26 89
Chapter 30 90

Genesis

Chapter 1

1-3 (Psalm 33:6, 9). A Reservoir of Means.—God spoke, and His words created His works in the natural world. God's creation is but a reservoir of means made ready for Him to employ instantly to do His pleasure (Letter 131, 1897).

26 (Ephesians 3:15). A Larger Family.—Infinite love—how great it is! God made the world to enlarge heaven. He desires a larger family of created intelligences (MS 78, 1901).

27 Man, a New and Distinct Order.—All heaven took a deep and joyful interest in the creation of the world and of man. Human beings were a new and distinct order. They were made "in the image of God," and it was the Creator's design that they should populate the earth (The Review and Herald, February 11, 1902).

29 (Psalm 104:14). Fruit in Our Hands.—The Lord has given His life to the trees and vines of His creation. His word can increase or decrease the fruit of the land. If men would open their understanding to discern the relation between nature and nature's God, faithful acknowledgments of the Creator's power would be heard. Without the life of God, nature would die. His creative works are dependent on Him. He bestows life-giving properties on all that nature produces. We are to regard the trees laden with fruit as the gift of God, just as much as though He placed the fruit in our hands (MS 114, 1899).

Chapter 2

2 (Exodus 20:8-11). Seven Literal Days.—The weekly cycle of seven literal days, six for labor, and the seventh for rest, which has been preserved and brought down through Bible history, originated in the great fact of the first seven days (Spiritual Gifts 3:90).

7 (1 Corinthians 3:9; Acts 17:28). Man Under God's Supervision.—The physical organism of man is under the supervision of God; but it is not like a clock, which is set in operation, and must go of itself. The heart beats, pulse succeeds pulse, breath succeeds breath, but the entire being is under the supervision of God. "Ye are God's husbandry, ye are God's building." In God we live and move and have our being. Each heart-beat, each breath, is the inspiration of Him who breathed into the nostrils of Adam the breath of life,—the inspiration of the ever-present God, the Great I AM (The Review and Herald, November 8, 1898).

(2 Peter 1:4). Partakers of God's Nature.—The Lord created man out of the dust of the earth. He made Adam a partaker of His life, His nature. There was breathed into him the breath of the Almighty, and he became a living soul. Adam was perfect in form—strong, comely, pure, bearing the image of his Maker (MS 102, 1903).

Physical Power Long Preserved.—Man came from the hand of his Creator perfect in organization and beautiful in form. The fact that he has for six thousand years withstood the ever-increasing weight of disease and crime is conclusive proof of the power of endurance with which he was first endowed (Christian Temperance and Bible Hygiene, 7).

8 Adam Crowned King in Eden.—Adam was crowned king in Eden. To him was given dominion over every living thing that God had created. The Lord blessed Adam and Eve with intelligence such as He had not given to any other creature. He made Adam the rightful sovereign over all the works of His hands. Man, made in the divine image, could contemplate and appreciate the glorious works of God in nature (Redemption; or the Temptation of Christ, page 7).

15 Eden, Heaven in Miniature.—Adam had themes for contemplation in the works of God in Eden, which was heaven in miniature. God did not form man merely to contemplate His glorious works; therefore, He gave him hands for labor, as well as a mind and heart for contemplation. If the happiness of man consisted in doing nothing, the Creator would not have given Adam his appointed work. Man was to find happiness in labor, as well as in meditation (Christian Temperance and Bible Hygiene, 7, 8).

16, 17 (Genesis 1:26; Isaiah 43:6, 7). To Re-populate Heaven After Test.—God created man for His own glory, that after test and trial the human family might become one with the heavenly family. It was God's purpose to re-populate heaven with the human family, if they would show themselves obedient to His every word. Adam was to be tested, to see whether he would be obedient, as the loyal angels, or disobedient. If he stood the test, his instruction to his children would have been only of loyalty. His mind and thoughts would have been as the mind and thoughts of God. He would have been taught by God as His husbandry and building. His character would have been moulded in accordance with the character of God (Letter 91, 1900).

17 (John 8:44; Genesis 3:4). Seeds of Death Satan's Work.—Christ never planted the seeds of death in the system. Satan planted these seeds when he tempted Adam to eat of the tree of knowledge which meant disobedience to God (MS 65, 1899) [published in F. D. Nichol, Ellen G. White and Her Critics].

(Revelation 13:8). Death Penalty Not Enforced at Once.—Adam listened to the words of the tempter, and yielding to his insinuations, fell into sin. Why was not the death penalty at once enforced in his case?—Because a ransom was found. God's only begotten Son volunteered to take the sin of man upon Himself, and to make an atonement for the fallen race. There could have been no pardon for sin had this atonement not been made. Had God pardoned Adam's sin without an atonement, sin would have been immortalized, and would have been perpetuated with a boldness that would have been without restraint (The Review and Herald, April 23, 1901).

Chapter 3

1-6 A Succession of Falls.—If the race had ceased to fall when Adam was driven from Eden, we should now be in a far more elevated condition physically, mentally, and morally. But while men deplore the fall of Adam, which has resulted in such unutterable woe, they disobey the express injunctions of God, as did Adam, although they have his example to warn them from doing as he did in violating the law of Jehovah. Would that man had stopped falling with Adam. But there has been a succession of falls. Men will not take warning from Adam's experience. They will indulge appetite and passion in direct violation of the law of God, and at the same time continue to mourn Adam's transgression, which brought sin into the world.

From Adam's day to ours there has been a succession of falls, each greater than the last, in every species of crime. God did not create a race of beings so devoid of health, beauty, and moral power as now exists in the world. Disease of every kind has been fearfully increasing upon the race. This has not been by God's especial providence, but directly contrary to His will. It has come by man's disregard of the very means which God has ordained to shield him from the terrible evils existing (The Review and Herald, March 4, 1875).

1 Satan Uses Instruments.—In Eden Satan used the serpent as his instrument. Today he makes use of the members of the human family, striving by means of every species of cunning and deception to hedge up the path of righteousness cast up for the ransomed of the Lord to walk in (Letter 91, 1900).

5 No Change in Satan's Propaganda.—God does not consult our opinions or preferences. He knows what human beings do not know,—the future results of every movement, and therefore our eyes should be directed to Him, and not to the worldly advantages presented by Satan. Satan tells us that if we give heed to him, we shall reach great heights of knowledge. Ye shall be as gods, he said to Eve, if you eat of the tree forbidden by God. The test given to Adam and Eve was very light, but they could not bear it. They disobeyed God, and this transgression opened the floodgates of woe on our world (MS 50, 1893).

6 Mildest Test Given.—With what intense interest the whole universe watched the conflict that was to decide the position of Adam and Eve. How attentively the angels listened to the words of Satan, the originator of sin, as he placed his own ideas above the commands of God, and sought to make of none effect the law of God through his deceptive reasoning! How anxiously they waited to see if the holy pair would be deluded by the tempter, and yield to his arts! They asked themselves, Will the holy pair transfer their faith and love from the Father and Son to Satan? Will they accept his falsehoods as truth? They knew that they might refrain from taking the fruit, and obey the positive injunction of God, or they might violate the express command of their Creator.

The mildest test was given them that could be given; for there was no need of their eating of the forbidden tree; everything that their wants required had been provided (BE July 24, 1899).

Gained Only a Knowledge of Sin and Its Results.—If Adam and Eve had never touched the forbidden tree, the Lord would have imparted to them knowledge,—knowledge upon which rested no curse of sin, knowledge that would have brought them everlasting joy. The only knowledge they gained by their disobedience was a knowledge of sin and its results ((Australasian) Union Conference Record, March 1, 1904).

Adam's Fall Inexplainable.—In what consisted the strength of the assault made upon Adam, which caused his fall? It was not indwelling sin; for God made Adam after His own character, pure and upright. There were no corrupt principles in the first Adam, no corrupt propensities or tendencies to evil. Adam was as faultless as the angels before God's throne. These things are inexplainable, but many things which now we cannot understand will be made plain when we shall see as we are seen, and know as we are known (Letter 191, 1899).

(Ecclesiastes 1:13-18).—Age after age, the curiosity of men has led them to seek for the tree of knowledge; and often they think they are plucking fruit most essential, when, like Solomon's research, they find it altogether vanity and nothingness in comparison with that science of true holiness which will open to them the gates of the city of God. The human ambition has been seeking for that kind of knowledge that will bring to them glory and self-exaltation and supremacy. Thus Adam and Eve were worked upon by Satan until God's restraint was snapped asunder, and their education under the teacher of lies began in order that they might have the knowledge which God had refused them,—to know the consequence of transgression (MS 67, 1898).

Fall Broke Golden Chain of Obedience.—Adam yielded to temptation and as we have the matter of sin and its consequence laid so distinctly before us, we can read from cause to effect and see the greatness of the act is not that which constitutes sin; but the disobedience of God's expressed will, which is a virtual denial of God, refusing the laws of His government....

The fall of our first parents broke the golden chain of implicit obedience of the human will to the divine. Obedience has no longer been deemed an absolute necessity. The human agents follow their own imaginations which the Lord said of the inhabitants of the old world was evil and that continually (MS 1, 1892).

Adam: Temptation Removed as Far as Possible.—The plan of salvation was so arranged that when Adam was tested, temptation was removed from him as far as possible. When Adam was tempted, he was not hungry (The Signs of the Times, April 4, 1900).

Man a Free Agent.—God had power to hold Adam back from touching the forbidden fruit; but had He done this, Satan would have been sustained in his charge against God's arbitrary rule. Man would not have been a free moral agent, but a mere machine (The Review and Herald, June 4, 1901).

Every Inducement to Remain Loyal.—It certainly was not God's purpose that man should be sinful. He made Adam pure and noble, with no tendency to evil. He placed him in Eden, where he had every inducement to remain loyal and obedient. The law was placed around him as a safeguard. (Ibid.).

7 Fig Leaves Will Not Cover Sin.—Adam and Eve both ate of the fruit, and obtained a knowledge which, had they obeyed God, they would never have had,—an experience in disobedience and disloyalty to God,—the knowledge that they were naked. The garment of innocence, a covering from God, which surrounded them, departed; and they supplied the place of this heavenly garment by sewing together fig-leaves for aprons.

This is the covering that the transgressors of the law of God have used since the days of Adam and Eve's disobedience. They have sewed together fig-leaves to cover their nakedness, caused by transgression. The fig-leaves represent the arguments used to cover disobedience. When the Lord calls the attention of men and women to the truth, the making of fig-leaves into aprons will be begun, to hide the nakedness of the soul. But the nakedness of the sinner is not covered. All the arguments pieced together by all who have interested themselves in this flimsy work will come to naught (The Review and Herald, November 15, 1898).

10, 11 Drew on Robes of Ignorance.—Had Adam and Eve never disobeyed their Creator, had they remained in the path of perfect rectitude, they could have known and understood God. But when they listened to the voice of the tempter, and sinned against God, the light of the garments of heavenly innocence departed from them; and in parting with the garments of innocence, they drew about them the dark robes of ignorance of God. The clear and perfect light that had hitherto surrounded them had lightened everything they approached; but deprived of that heavenly light, the posterity of Adam could no longer trace the character of God in His created works (The Review and Herald, March 17, 1904).

15 Adam Knew Original Law.—Adam and Eve at their creation had knowledge of the original law of God. It was imprinted upon their hearts, and they were acquainted with the claims of law upon them. When they transgressed the law of God, and fell from their state of happy innocence, and became sinners, the future of the fallen race was not relieved by a single ray of hope. God pitied them, and Christ devised the plan for their salvation by Himself bearing the guilt. When the curse was pronounced upon the earth and upon man, in connection with the curse was a promise that through Christ there was hope and pardon for the transgression of God's law. Although gloom and darkness hung, like the pall of death, over the future, yet in the promise of the Redeemer, the Star of hope lighted up the dark future. The gospel was first preached to Adam by Christ. Adam and Eve felt sincere sorrow and repentance for their guilt. They believed the precious promise of God, and were saved from utter ruin (The Review and Herald, April 29, 1875).

Christ the Immediate Surety.—As soon as there was sin, there was a Saviour. Christ knew that He would have to suffer, yet He became man's substitute. As soon as Adam sinned, the Son of God presented Himself as surety for the human race, with just as much power to avert the doom pronounced upon the guilty as when He died upon the cross of Calvary (The Review and Herald, March 12, 1901).

Continent of Heaven.—Jesus became the world's Redeemer, rendering perfect obedience to every word that proceedeth out of the mouth of God. He redeemed Adam's disgraceful fall, uniting the earth, that had been divorced from God by sin, to the continent of heaven [Obviously the word "continent" is here employed in a broader sense than is commonly understood today. It is in keeping with usage now obsolete, which permitted the word "continent" to apply to "the 'solid globe' or orb of the sun or moon" (See Oxford English Dictionary).—Editor.] (Be aug. 6, 1894).

Connected With Sphere of Glory.—Though earth was struck off from the continent of heaven [Obviously the word "continent" is here employed in a broader sense than is commonly understood today. It is in keeping with usage now obsolete, which permitted the word "continent" to apply to "the 'solid globe' or orb of the sun or moon" (See Oxford English Dictionary).—Editor.] and alienated from its communion, Jesus has connected it again with the sphere of glory (st nov. 24, 1887).

Instantaneous Substitution.—The instant man accepted the temptations of Satan, and did the very things God had said he should not do, Christ, the Son of God, stood between the living and the dead, saying, "Let the punishment fall on Me. I will stand in man's place. He shall have another chance" (Letter, February 13, 1900, p. 22).

Christ Placed Feet in Adam's Steps.—What love! What amazing condescension! The King of glory proposed to humble Himself to fallen humanity! He would place His feet in Adam's steps. He would take man's fallen nature, and engage to cope with the strong foe who triumphed over Adam. He would overcome Satan, and in thus doing He would open the way for the redemption from the disgrace of Adam's failure and fall, of all those who would believe on Him (Redemption; or the Temptation of Christ in The Wilderness, 15).

16, 17 Execution of Sentence Withheld.—God forbears, for a time, the full execution of the sentence of death pronounced upon man. Satan flattered himself that he had forever broken the link between heaven and earth. But in this he was greatly mistaken and disappointed. The Father had given the world into the hands of His Son for Him to redeem from the curse and the disgrace of Adam's failure and fall (Redemption; or the Temptation of Christ in The Wilderness, 17).

17, 18 The Curse on All Creation.—All nature is confused; for God forbade the earth to carry out the purpose He had originally designed for it. Let there be no peace to the wicked, saith the Lord. The curse of God is upon all creation. Every year it makes itself more decidedly felt (MS 76a, 1901).

The first curse was pronounced upon the posterity of Adam and upon the earth, because of disobedience. The second curse came upon the ground after Cain slew his brother Abel. The third most dreadful curse from God, came upon the earth at the Flood (Spiritual Gifts 4a:121).

The land has felt the curse, more and more heavily. Before the Flood, the first leaf which fell, and was discovered decaying upon the ground, caused those who feared God great sorrow. They mourned over it as we mourn over the loss of a dead friend. In the decaying leaf they could see an evidence of the curse, and of the decay of nature (Spiritual Gifts 4a:155).

(Romans 8:22).—The sin of man has brought the sure result,—decay, deformity, and death. Today the whole world is tainted, corrupted, stricken with mortal disease. The earth groaneth under the continual transgression of the inhabitants thereof (Letter, February 13, 1900, p. 22).

The Lord's curse is upon the earth, upon man, upon beast, upon the fish in the sea, and as transgression becomes almost universal the curse will be permitted to become as broad and as deep as the transgression (Letter 59, 1898).

Tokens of God's Continued Love.—After the transgression of Adam, God might have destroyed every opening bud and blooming flower, or He might have taken away their fragrance, so grateful to the senses. In the earth seared and marred by the curse, in the briers, the thistles, the thorns, the tares, we may read the law of condemnation; but in the delicate color and perfume of the flowers, we may learn that God still loves us, that His mercy is not wholly withdrawn from the earth (The Review and Herald, November 8, 1898).

17-19—God said to Adam, and to all the descendants of Adam, In the sweat of thy face shalt thou eat bread; for from henceforth the earth must be worked under the drawback of transgression. Thorns and briars shall it produce (MS 84, 1897).

There is no place upon earth where the track of the serpent is not seen and his venomous sting felt. The whole earth is defiled under the inhabitants thereof. The curse is increasing as transgression increases (Letter, February 13, 1900, p. 22).

18 Amalgamation Brought Noxious Plants.—Not one noxious plant was placed in the Lord's great garden, but after Adam and Eve sinned, poisonous herbs sprang up. In the parable of the sower the question was asked the Master, "Didst not thou sow good seed in thy field? how then hath it tares?" The Master answered, "An enemy hath done this." All tares are sown by the evil one. Every noxious herb is of his sowing, and by his ingenious methods of amalgamation he has corrupted the earth with tares (MS 65, 1899) [published in F. D. Nichol, Ellen G. White and Her Critics].

22-24 (Revelation 22:2, 14). Obedience Is Condition of Eating of Tree.—Transgression of God's requirements excluded Adam from the Garden of Eden. A flaming sword was placed around the tree of life, lest man should put forth his hand and partake of it, immortalizing sin. Obedience to all the commandments of God was the condition of eating of the tree of life. Adam fell by disobedience, forfeiting by sin all right to use either the life-giving fruit of the tree in the midst of the Garden, or its leaves, which are for the healing of the nations.

Obedience through Jesus Christ gives to man perfection of character and a right to that tree of life. The conditions of again partaking of the fruit of the tree are plainly stated in the testimony of Jesus Christ to John: "Blessed are they that do His commandments, that they may have right to the tree of life, and many enter in through the gates into the city" (MS 72, 1901).

24 (Matthew 4:4; 6:63). No Sword Before Our Tree of Life.—The Scriptures, "It is written," is the gospel we are to preach. No flaming sword is placed before this tree of life. All who will may partake of it. There is no power that can prohibit any soul from taking of the fruit of this tree of life. All may eat and live forever (Letter 20, 1900).

Chapter 4

4 Offering Must Be Sprinkled With Blood.—In every offering to God we are to acknowledge the one great Gift; that alone can make our service acceptable to him. When Abel offered the firstling of the flock, he acknowledged God, not only as the Giver of his temporal blessings, but also as the Giver of the Saviour. Abel's gift was the very choicest he could bring; for it was the Lord's specified claim. But Cain brought only of the fruit of the ground, and his offering was not accepted by the Lord. It did not express faith in Christ. All our offerings must be sprinkled with the blood of the atonement. As the purchased possession of the Son of God, we are to give the Lord our own individual lives (The Review and Herald, November 24, 1896).

(Genesis 2:17). **Substitute Accepted for Time Being.**—Fallen man, because of his guilt, could no longer come directly before God with his supplications; for his transgression of the divine law had placed an impassable barrier between the holy God and the transgressor. But a plan was devised that the sentence of death should rest upon a substitute. In the plan of redemption there must be the shedding of blood, for death must come in consequence of man's sin. The beasts for sacrificial offerings were to prefigure Christ. In the slain victim, man was to see the fulfillment for the time being of God's word, "Ye shall surely die" (Redemption; or the Temptation of Christ, p. 19).

6 God Marks Every Action.—The Lord saw the wrath of Cain, He saw the falling of his countenance. Thus is revealed how closely the Lord marks every action, all the intents and purposes, yes, even the expression of the countenance. This, though man may say nothing, expresses his refusal to do the way and will of God.... Well might the question be asked you of the Lord, when you cannot follow the impulse of your own rebellious heart, and are restrained from doing your own unrighteous, unsanctified will, "Why art thou wroth? and why is thy countenance fallen?" Such exhibitions reveal that because they cannot do after Satan's arts and devices they are provoked, and can only manifest a spirit similar to that of Cain (MS 77, 1897).

8 Contention Must Come.—There could be no harmony between the two brothers, and contention must come. Abel could not concede to Cain without being guilty of disobedience to the special commands of God (Letter 16, 1897).

Cain Filled With Doubt and Madness.—Satan is the parent of unbelief, murmuring, and rebellion. He filled Cain with doubt and with madness against his innocent brother and against God, because his sacrifice was refused and Abel's accepted. And he slew his brother in his insane madness (The Review and Herald, March 3, 1874).

15 Mark of Cain.—God has given to every man his work; and if any one turns from the work that God has given him, to do the work of Satan, to defile his own body or lead another into sin, that man's work is cursed, and the brand of Cain is placed upon him. The ruin of his victim will cry unto God, as did the blood of Abel (The Review and Herald, March 6, 1894).

Any man, be he minister or layman, who seeks to compel or control the reason of any other man, becomes an agent of Satan, to do his work, and in the sight of the heavenly universe he bears the mark of Cain (MS 29, 1911).

25 Seth More Noble in Stature Than Cain or Abel.—Seth was of more noble stature than Cain or Abel, and resembled Adam more than any of his other sons. The descendants of Seth had separated themselves from the wicked descendants of Cain. They cherished the knowledge of God's will, while the ungodly race of Cain had no respect for God and His sacred commandments (Spiritual Gifts 3:60).

Chapter 5

22-24 Enoch Saw God Only by Faith.—Did he [Enoch] see God by his side? Only by faith. He knew that the Lord was there, and he adhered steadfastly to the principles of truth. We, too, are to walk with God. When we do this, our faces will be lighted up by the brightness of His presence, and when we meet one another, we shall speak of His power, saying, Praise God. Good is the Lord, and good is the word of the Lord (MS 17, 1903).

Christ a Constant Companion.—We can have what Enoch had. We can have Christ as our constant companion. Enoch walked with God, and when assailed by the tempter, he could talk with God about it. He had no "It is written" as we have, but he had a knowledge of his heavenly Companion. He made God his Counsellor, and was closely bound up with Jesus. And Enoch was honored in this course. He was translated to heaven without seeing death. And those who will be translated at the close of time, will be those who commune with God on earth. Those who make manifest that their life is hid with Christ in God will ever be representing Him in all their life-practices. Selfishness will be cut out by the roots (MS 38, 1897).

Strove to Conform to Divine Likeness.—Let us realize the weakness of humanity, and see where man fails in his self-sufficiency. We shall then be filled with a desire to be just what God desires us to be,—pure, noble, sanctified. We shall hunger and thirst after the righteousness of Christ. To be like God will be the one desire of the soul.

This is the desire that filled Enoch's heart. And we read that he walked with God. He studied the character of God to a purpose. He did not mark out his own course, or set up his own will, as if he thought himself fully qualified to manage matters. He strove to conform himself to the divine likeness (Letter 169, 1903).

How Enoch Walked With God.—While trusting in your heavenly Father for the help you need, He will not leave you. God has a heaven full of blessings that He wants to bestow on those who are earnestly seeking for that help which the Lord alone can give. It was in looking in faith to Jesus, in asking of Him, in believing that every word spoken would be verified, that Enoch walked with God. He kept close by the side of God, obeying His every word.... His was a wonderful life of oneness. Christ was his Companion. He was in intimate fellowship with God (MS 111, 1898).

Abode in Pure Atmosphere.—He [Enoch] did not make his abode with the wicked. He did not locate in Sodom, thinking to save Sodom. He placed himself and his family where the atmosphere would be as pure as possible. Then at times he went forth to the inhabitants of the world with his God-given message. Every visit he made to the world was painful to him. He saw and understood something of the leprosy of sin. After proclaiming his message, he always took back with him to his place of retirement some who had received the warning. Some of these became overcomers, and died before the Flood came. But some had lived so long in the corrupting influence of sin that they could not endure righteousness (MS 42, 1900).

24 No Moral Darkness So Dense.—Enoch walked with God, while of the world around him sacred history records, "And God saw that the wickedness of man was great in the earth, and that every imagination of the thoughts of his heart was only evil continually." Enoch's righteous life was in marked contrast with the wicked people around him. His piety, his purity, his unswerving integrity were the result of his walking with God, while the wickedness of the world was the result of their walking with the deceiver of mankind. There never has been and never will be an age when the moral darkness will be so dense as when Enoch lived a life of irreproachable righteousness (MS 43, 1900).

Enoch the First Prophet.—Enoch was the first prophet among mankind. He foretold by prophecy the second coming of Christ to our world, and his work at that time. His life was a specimen of Christian consistency. Holy lips alone should speak forth the words of God in denunciation and judgments. His prophecy is not found in the writings of the Old Testament. We may never find any books which relate to the works of Enoch, but Jude, a prophet of God, mentions the work of Enoch (Ibid.).

Chapter 6

2 Co-operation With God Avoids Cain-worship.—Had man co-operated with God, there would have been no Cain-worshipers. Abel's example of obedience would have been followed. Men might have worked out the will of God. They might have obeyed His law, and in obedience they would have found salvation. God and the heavenly universe would have helped them to retain the divine likeness. Longevity would have been preserved; and God would have delighted in the work of His hands (The Review and Herald, December 27, 1898).

3 (1 Peter 3:18-21). God Preached Through Methuselah, Noah, and Others.—God granted them one hundred and twenty years of probation, and during that time preached to them through Methuselah, Noah, and many others of His servants. Had they listened to the testimony of these faithful witnesses, had they repented and returned to their loyalty, God would not have destroyed them (The Review and Herald, April 23, 1901).

Enoch Bore Testimony Unflinchingly.—Before the destruction of the antediluvian world, Enoch bore his testimony unflinchingly (The Review and Herald, November 1, 1906).

Voices of Noah and Methuselah Heard.—God determined to purify the world by a flood; but in mercy and love He gave the antediluvians a probation of one hundred and twenty years. During this time, while the ark was building, the voices of Noah, Methuselah, and many others were heard in warning and entreaty, and every blow struck on the ark was a warning message (The Review and Herald, September 19, 1907).

Some Believed; Some Backslid.—For one hundred and twenty years Noah proclaimed the message of warning to the antediluvian world; but only a few repented. Some of the carpenters he employed in building the ark believed the message, but died before the Flood; others of Noah's converts backslid (MS 65, 1906).

Many of the believing ones kept the faith, and died triumphant (MS 35, 1906).

Enoch's Experience a Convincing Sermon.—[Jude 14, 15 quoted.] The sermon preached by Enoch, and his translation to heaven was a convincing argument to all living in Enoch's time. It was an argument that Methuselah and Noah could use with power to show that the righteous could be translated (MS 46, 1895).

Association With Unbelievers Caused Loss.—Those who believed when Noah began to build the ark, lost their faith through association with unbelievers who aroused all the old passion for amusement and display (The Review and Herald, September 15, 1904).

(1 John 3:8). **Christ in Warfare in Noah's Day.**—"For this purpose the Son of God was manifested, that He might destroy the works of the devil." Christ was engaged in this warfare in Noah's day. It was His voice that spoke to the inhabitants of the old world in messages of warning, reproof, and invitation. He gave the people a probation of one hundred and twenty years, in which they might have repented. But they chose the deceptions of Satan, and perished in the waters of the Flood (The Review and Herald, March 12, 1901).

4 Great Art and Inventions Perished.—There perished in the Flood greater inventions of art and human skill than the world knows of today. The arts destroyed were more than the boasted arts of today (Letter 65, 1898).

How did man gain his knowledge of how to devise?—From the Lord, by studying the formation and habits of different animals. Every animal is a lesson book, and from the use they make of their bodies and the weapons provided them, men have learned to make apparatus for every kind of work. If men could only know how many arts have been lost to our world, they would not talk so fluently of the dark ages. Could they have seen how God once worked through His human subjects, they would speak with less confidence of the arts of the antediluvian world. More was lost in the Flood, in many ways, than men today know. Looking upon the world, God saw that the intellect He had given man was perverted, that the imagination of his heart was evil and that continually. God had given these men knowledge. He had given them valuable ideas, that they might carry out His plan. But the Lord saw that those whom He designed should possess wisdom, tact, and judgment, were using every quality of the mind to glorify self. By the waters of the Flood, He blotted this long-lived race from the earth, and with them perished the knowledge they had used only for evil. When the earth was repeopled, the Lord trusted His wisdom more sparingly to men, giving them only the ability they would need in carrying out His great plan (Letter 175, 1896).

Delusions of Progress.—True knowledge has decreased with every successive generation. God is infinite, and the first people upon the earth received their instructions from that infinite God who created the world. Those who received their knowledge direct from infinite wisdom were not deficient in knowledge.

God instructed Noah how to make that immense ark, for the saving of himself and his family. He also instructed Moses how to make the tabernacle, and the embroidery, and skillful work which was to adorn the sanctuary. The women wrought, with great ingenuity the embroidery of silver and gold. Skillful men were not wanting to accomplish the work of making the ark, the tabernacle, and the vessels of solid gold.

God gave David a pattern of the temple which Solomon built. None but the most skillful men of design and art were allowed to have anything to do with the work. Every stone for the temple was prepared to exactly fill its place, before being brought to the temple. And the temple came together without the sound of an axe or hammer. There is no such building to be found in the world for beauty, richness and splendor.

There are many inventions and improvements, and labor-saving machines now that the ancients did not have. They did not need them....

The greater the length of time the earth has lain under the curse, the more difficult has it been for man to cultivate it, and make it productive. As the soil has become more barren, and double labor has had to be expended upon it, God has raised up men with inventive faculties to construct implements to lighten labor on the land groaning under the curse. But God has not been in all man's inventions. Satan has controlled the minds of men to a great extent, and has hurried men to new inventions which has led them to forget God.

In strength of intellect, men who now live can bear no comparison to the ancients. There have been more ancient arts lost than the present generation now possess. For skill and art those living in this degenerate age will not compare with the knowledge possessed by strong men who lived near one thousand years.

Men before the Flood lived many hundreds of years, and when one hundred years old they were considered but youths. Those long-lived men had sound minds in sound bodies. Their mental and physical strength was so great that the present feeble generation can bear no comparison to them. Those ancients had nearly one thousand years in which to acquire knowledge. They came upon the stage of action from the ages of sixty to one hundred years, about the time those who now live the longest have acted their part in their little short life time, and have passed off the stage. Those who are deceived, and flattered on in the delusion that the present is an age of real progress, and that the human race has been in ages past progressing in true knowledge, are under the influence of the father of lies, whose work has ever been to turn the truth of God into a lie (4SG 154-156).

Giants Before the Flood.—At the first resurrection all come forth in immortal bloom, but at the second, the marks of the curse are visible upon all. All come up as they went down into their graves. Those who lived before the Flood, come forth with their giant-like stature, more than twice as tall as men now living upon the earth, and well proportioned. The generations after the Flood were less in stature (Spiritual Gifts 3:84).

5 Degenerated From Lightness to Debasing Sins.—We have the history of the antediluvians, and of the cities of the plain, whose course of conduct degenerated from lightness and frivolity to debasing sins that called down the wrath of God in a most dreadful destruction, in order to rid the earth of the curse of their contaminating influence. Inclination and passion bore sway over reason. Self was their god, and the knowledge of the Most High was nearly obliterated through the selfish indulgence of corrupt passions (Letter 74, 1896).

Perverted What Was Lawful.—The sin of the antediluvians was in perverting that which in itself was lawful. They corrupted God's gifts by using them to minister to their selfish desires. The indulgence of appetite and base passion made their imaginations altogether corrupt. The antediluvians were slaves of Satan, led and controlled by him (MS 24, 1891).

Corrupted Through Perverted Appetite.—The inhabitants of the Noachian world were destroyed, because they were corrupted through the indulgence of perverted appetite (The Signs of the Times, September 2, 1875).

11 Worshiped Self-indulgence; Fostered Crime.—They worshipped selfish indulgence,—eating, drinking, merry-making,—and resorted to acts of violence and crime if their desires and passions were interfered with.

In the days of Noah the overwhelming majority was opposed to the truth, and enamored with a tissue of falsehoods. The land was filled with violence. War, crime, murder, was the order of the day. Just so will it be before Christ's second coming (MS 24, 1891).

12, 13 Noah Ridiculed.—Before the destruction of the old world by a flood, there were talented men, men who possessed skill and knowledge. But they became corrupt in their imagination, because they left God out of their plans and councils. They were wise to do what God had never told them to do, wise to do evil. The Lord saw that this example would be deleterious to those who should afterwards be born, and He took the matter in hand. For one hundred twenty years He sent them warnings through His servant Noah. But they used the probation so graciously granted them in ridiculing Noah. They caricatured him and criticized him. They laughed at him for his peculiar earnestness and intense feeling in regard to the judgments which he declared God would surely fulfill. They talked of science and of the laws controlling nature. Then they held a carnival over the words of Noah, calling him a crazy fanatic. God's patience was exhausted. He said to Noah, "The end of all flesh is come before me; for the earth is filled with violence through them, and, behold, I will destroy them from the earth" (MS 29, 1890).

17 (2 Peter 3:10; Revelation 14:10). Coal and Oil Agencies in Final Destruction.—Those majestic trees which God had caused to grow upon the earth, for the benefit of the inhabitants of the old world, and which they had used to form into idols, and to corrupt themselves with, God has reserved in the earth, in the shape of coal and oil to use as agencies in their final destruction. As He called forth the waters in the earth at the time of the Flood, as weapons from His arsenal to accomplish the destruction of the antediluvian race, so at the end of the one thousand years He will call forth the fires in the earth as His weapons which He has reserved for the final destruction, not only of successive generations since the Flood, but the antediluvian race who perished by the Flood (Spiritual Gifts 3:87).

Chapter 7

21-23 Kept Through Faith in Christ.—It was Christ who kept the ark safe amid the roaring, seething billows, because its inmates had faith in His power to preserve them (The Review and Herald, March 12, 1901).

Chapter 8

13 Seeds and Some Plants Preserved.—The beautiful trees and shrubbery bearing flowers were destroyed, yet Noah preserved seed and took it with him in the ark, and God by His miraculous power preserved a few of the different kinds of trees and shrubs alive for future generations. Soon after the Flood trees and plants seemed to spring out of the very rocks. In God's providence seeds were scattered and driven into the crevices of the rocks and there securely hid for the future use of man (Spiritual Gifts 3:76).

Chapter 9

6 God Protects Man's Rights.—How carefully God protects the rights of men! He has attached a penalty to wilful murder. "Whoso sheddeth man's blood, by man shall his blood be shed." (Genesis 9:6) If one murderer were permitted to go unpunished, he would by his evil influence and cruel violence subvert others. This would result in a condition of things similar to that which existed before the Flood. God must punish murderers. He gives life, and He will take life, if that life becomes a terror and a menace (MS 126, 1901).

12 Bow Shows Christ's Love Which Encircles Earth.—As we look upon this bow, the seal and sign of God's promise to man, that the tempest of His wrath should no more desolate our world by the waters of a flood, we contemplate that other than finite eyes are looking upon this glorious sight. Angels rejoice as they gaze upon this precious token of God's love to man. The world's Redeemer looks upon it; for it was through His instrumentality that this bow was made to appear in the heavens, as a token or covenant of promise to man. God Himself looks upon the bow in the clouds, and remembers His everlasting covenant between Himself and man.

After the fearful exhibition of God's avenging power, in the destruction of the Old World by a flood, had passed, He knew that those who had been saved from the general ruin would have their fears awakened whenever the clouds should gather, the thunders roll, and the lightnings flash; and that the sound of the tempest and the pouring out of the waters from the heavens would strike terror to their hearts, for fear that another flood was coming upon them. But behold the love of God in the promise: [Genesis 9:12-15 quoted].

The family of Noah looked with admiration and reverential awe mingled with joy upon this sign of God's mercy, which spanned the heavens. The bow represents Christ's love which encircles the earth, and reaches unto the highest heavens, connecting men with God, and linking earth with heaven.

As we gaze upon the beautiful sight, we may be joyful in God, assured that He Himself is looking upon this token of His covenant, and that as He looks upon it

He remembers the children of earth, to whom it was given. Their afflictions, perils, and trials are not hidden from Him. We may rejoice in hope, for the bow of God's covenant is over us. He never will forget the children of His care. How difficult for the mind of finite man to take in the peculiar love and tenderness of God, and His matchless condescension when He said, "I will look upon the bow in the cloud, and remember thee" (The Review and Herald, February 26, 1880).

Chapter 11

2-9 Men Resumed Hostility.—But no sooner was the earth repeopled than men resumed their hostility to God and heaven. They transmitted their enmity to their posterity, as though the art and device of misleading men, and causing them to continue the unnatural warfare, was a sacred legacy (Letter 4, 1896).

3-7 Confederacy Born of Rebellion.—This confederacy was born of rebellion against God. The dwellers on the plain of Shinar established their kingdom for self-exaltation, not for the glory of God. Had they succeeded, a mighty power would have borne sway, banishing righteousness, and inaugurating a new religion. The world would have been demoralized. The mixture of religious ideas with erroneous theories would have resulted in closing the door to peace, happiness, and security. These suppositions, erroneous theories, carried out and perfected, would have directed minds from allegiance to the divine statutes, and the law of Jehovah would have been ignored and forgotten. Determined men, inspired and urged on by the first great rebel, would have resisted any interference with their plans or their evil course. In the place of the divine precepts they would have substituted laws framed in accordance with the desires of their selfish hearts, in order that they might carry out their purposes (The Review and Herald, December 10, 1903).

Chapter 12

1 Abraham Chosen From Idolatrous Generation.—After the Flood the people once more increased on the earth, and wickedness also increased. Idolatry became well-nigh universal, and the Lord finally left the hardened transgressors to follow their evil ways, while He chose Abraham, of the line of Shem, and made him the keeper of His law for future generations (MS 65, 1906).

Abraham's Family Touched by False Worship.—In that age, idolatry was fast creeping in and conflicting with the worship of the true God. But Abraham did not become an idolater. Although his own father was vacillating between the true and the false worship, and with his knowledge of the truth false theories and idolatrous practises were mingled, Abraham kept free from this infatuation. He was not ashamed of his faith, and made no effort to hide the fact that he made God his trust. He "builded an altar unto the Lord, and called upon the name of the Lord" (The Youth's Instructor, March 4, 1897).

2, 3 (John 8:56; Galatians 3:8). Abraham Saw Coming Redeemer.—Christ said to the Pharisees, "Your father Abraham rejoiced to see my day: and he saw it, and was glad" (John 8:56). How did Abraham know of the coming of the Redeemer? God gave him light in regard to the future. He looked forward to the time when the Saviour should come to this earth, His divinity veiled by humanity. By faith he saw the world's Redeemer coming as God in the flesh. He saw the weight of guilt lifted from the human race, and borne by the divine substitute (MS 33, 1911).

(Ephesians 2:8). Keep Commandments Under Abrahamic Covenant.—If it were not possible for human beings under the Abrahamic covenant to keep the commandments of God, every soul of us is lost. The Abrahamic covenant is the covenant of grace. "By grace ye are saved." [John 1:11, 12 quoted.] Disobedient children? No, obedient to all His commandments. If it were not possible for us to be commandment-keepers, then why does He make the obedience to His commandments the proof that we love Him? (Letter 16, 1892).

Chapter 13

10, 11 Lot Went in Rich; Came Out With Nothing.—He [Lot] chose a land which was beautiful in situation, which promised great returns. Lot went in rich, and came forth with nothing as the result of his choice. It makes every difference whether men place themselves in positions where they will have the very best help of correct influences, or whether they choose temporal advantages. There are many ways which lead to Sodom. We all need anointed eyesight, that we may discern the way that leads to God (Letter 109, 1899).

Lot Was Convinced of Mistake.—Lot chose Sodom for his home because he saw advantages to be gained there from a worldly point of view. But after he had established himself, and grown rich in earthly treasure, he was convinced that he had made a mistake in not taking into consideration the moral standing of the community in which he was to make his home (The Review and Herald, November 14, 1882).

Chapter 14

18-20 Melchizedek, Christ's Representative.—God has never left Himself without witness on the earth. At one time Melchisedek represented the Lord Jesus Christ in person, to reveal the truth of heaven, and perpetuate the law of God (Letter 190, 1905).

It was Christ that spoke through Melchisedek, the priest of the most high God. Melchisedek was not Christ, but he was the voice of God in the world, the representative of the Father. And all through the generations of the past, Christ has spoken; Christ has led His people, and has been the light of the world. When God chose Abraham as a representative of His truth, He took him out of his country, and away from his kindred, and set him apart. He desired to mold him after His own model. He desired to teach him according to His own plan (The Review and Herald, February 18, 1890).

20 (Genesis 28:22; Leviticus 27:30). Tithing Goes Back to Days of Adam.—The tithing system reaches back beyond the days of Moses. Men were required to offer to God gifts for religious purposes, before the definite system was given to Moses, even as far back as the days of Adam. In complying with God's requirements they were to manifest in offerings their appreciation of His mercies and blessings to them. This was continued through successive generations, and was carried out by Abraham, who gave tithes to Melchisedek, the priest of the most high God. The same principle existed in the days of Job (The Signs of the Times, April 29, 1875).

Chapter 15

9-11 Let Nothing Mar Your Sacrifice.—Watch as faithfully as did Abraham lest the ravens or any birds of prey alight upon your sacrifice and offering to God. Every thought of doubt should be so guarded that it will not see the light of day by utterance. Light always flees from words which honor the powers of darkness (Letter 7, 1892).

16 God Bore Long for Sake of Good Amorites.—In the days of Abraham the Lord declared, "The iniquity of the Amorites is not yet full." He would not at that time allow them to be destroyed. In this is revealed the long-sufferance of God. The Amorites were at enmity against His law; they believed not in Him as the true and living God; but among them were a few good persons, and for the sake of these few, He forbore long. Centuries afterward, when the Israelites returned from Egypt to the promised land, the Amorites were "cast out before the children of Israel." They finally suffered calamity because of continued willful disregard of the law of God (The Review and Herald, July 12, 1906).

(Ecclesiastes 8:11, 12). Rejection of Light Led to Destruction of Amorites.—The Amorites were inhabitants of Canaan, and the Lord had promised the land of Canaan to the Israelites; but a long interval must pass before His people should possess the land. He stated the reason why this interval must pass. He told them that the iniquity of the Amorites was not yet full, and their expulsion and extermination could not be justified until they had filled up the cup of their iniquity. Idolatry and sin marked their course, but the measure of their guilt was not such that they could be devoted to destruction. In His love and pity God would let light shine upon them in more distinct rays; He would give them opportunity to behold the working of His wondrous power, that there might be no excuse for their course of evil. It is thus that God deals with the nations. Through a certain period of probation He exercises long-suffering toward nations, cities, and individuals. But when it is evident that they will not come unto Him that they might have life, judgments are visited upon them. The time came when judgment was inflicted upon the Amorites, and the time will come when all the transgressors of His law will know that God will by no means clear the guilty (The Review and Herald, May 2, 1893).

Chapter 18

19 Fulfilling Conditions Brings Blessing.—If parents would fulfill the conditions upon which God has promised to be their strength, they would not fail of receiving His blessing in their households (The Review and Herald, May 21, 1895).

Chapter 19

12-14 Sodom Passed Boundary of Mercy.—The Sodomites had passed the boundary of mercy, and no more light was granted to them prior to their destruction. Had the warning gone through these cities of the plain, and had they been told just what was to come, who of them would have believed it? They would no more have accepted the message, and God knew it, than the sons-in-law of Lot (MS 19a, 1886).

16. Lot Paralyzed.—Lot was paralyzed by the great calamity about to occur; he was stupefied with grief at the thought of leaving all he held dear on earth (The Review and Herald, November 14, 1882).

Chapter 22

1 (James 1:13). God Permitted Circumstances to Test.—What is temptation?—It is the means by which those who claim to be the children of God are tested and tried. We read that God tempted Abraham, that He tempted the children of Israel. This means that He permitted circumstances to occur to test their faith, and lead them to look to Him for help. God permits temptation to come to His people today, that they may realize that He is their helper. If they draw nigh to Him when they are tempted, He strengthens them to meet the temptation. But if they yield to the enemy, neglecting to place themselves close to their Almighty Helper, they are overcome. They separate themselves from God. They do not give evidence that they walk in God's way (The Signs of the Times, March 12, 1912).

2 Nothing Too Precious to Give to God.—This act of faith in Abraham is recorded for our benefit. It teaches us the great lesson of confidence in the requirements of God, however close and cutting they may be; and it teaches children perfect submission to their parents and to God. By Abraham's obedience we are taught that nothing is too precious for us to give to God (The Signs of the Times, January 27, 1887).

12 Every Gift Is the Lord's.—Abraham's test was the most severe that could come to a human being. Had he failed under it, he would never have been registered as the father of the faithful. Had he deviated from God's command, the world would have lost an inspiring example of unquestioning faith and obedience. The lesson was given to shine down through the ages, that we may learn that there is nothing too precious to be given to God. It is when we look upon every gift as the Lord's, to be used in His service, that we secure the heavenly benediction. Give back to God your intrusted possession, and more will be intrusted to you. Keep your possessions to yourself, and you will receive no reward in this life, and will lose the reward of the life to come (The Youth's Instructor, June 6, 1901).

Isaac a Figure of Christ.—The offering of Isaac was designed by God to prefigure the sacrifice of His Son. Isaac was a figure of the Son of God, who was offered a sacrifice for the sins of the world. God desired to impress upon Abraham the gospel of salvation to men; and in order to make the truth a reality, and to test his faith, He required Abraham to slay his darling Isaac. All the agony that Abraham endured during that dark and fearful trial was for the purpose of deeply impressing upon his understanding the plan of redemption for fallen man (The Youth's Instructor, March 1, 1900).

Chapter 25

29-34 (Hebrews 12:16, 17). Birthright Lost Value and Sacredness.—Esau had a special, strong desire for a particular article of food, and he had gratified self so long that he did not feel the necessity of turning from the tempting, coveted dish. He thought upon it, and made no special effort to restrain his appetite, until its power bore down every other consideration, and controlled him, and he imagined he would suffer great inconvenience, and even death, if he could not have that particular dish. The more he thought upon it, the more his desire strengthened, until his birthright, which was sacred, lost its value and its sacredness. He thought, Well, if I now sell it, I can easily buy it back again.... When he sought to purchase it back, even at a great sacrifice on his part, he was not able to do so.... He sought for repentance carefully and with tears. It was all in vain. He had despised the blessing, and the Lord removed it from him forever (The Review and Herald, April 27, 1886).

Esau a Type.—Esau passed the crisis of his life without knowing it. What he regarded as a matter worthy of scarcely a thought was the act which revealed the prevailing traits of his character. It showed his choice, showed his true estimate of that which was sacred and which should have been sacredly cherished. He sold his birthright for a small indulgence to meet his present wants, and this determined the after course of his life. To Esau a morsel of meat was more than the service of his Master (Letter 5, 1877).

Esau represents those who have not tasted of the privileges which are theirs, purchased for them at infinite cost, but have sold their birthright for some gratification of appetite, or for the love of gain (Letter 4, 1898).

Chapter 28

12 Those Who Mount Must Place Feet Firmly.—Jesus is the ladder to heaven, ...and God calls upon us to mount this ladder. But we cannot do this while we load ourselves down with earthly treasures. We wrong ourselves when we place our convenience and personal advantages before the things of God. There is no salvation in earthly possessions or surroundings. A man is not exalted in God's sight, or accredited by Him as possessing goodness, because he has earthly riches. If we gain a genuine experience in climbing, we shall learn that as we ascend we must leave every hindrance behind. Those who mount must place their feet firmly on every round of the ladder (The Signs of the Times, February 1, 1899).

12, 13 Christ Bridges the Gulf.—Jacob thought to gain a right to the birthright through deception, but he found himself disappointed. He thought he had lost everything, his connection with God, his home, and all, and there he was a disappointed fugitive. But what did God do? He looked upon him in his hopeless condition, He saw his disappointment, and He saw there was material there that would render back glory to God. No sooner does He see his condition than He presents the mystic ladder, which represents Jesus Christ. Here is man, who had lost all connection with God, and the God of heaven looks upon him and consents that Christ shall bridge the gulf which sin has made. We might have looked and said, I long for heaven but how can I reach it? I see no way. That is what Jacob thought, and so God shows him the vision of the ladder, and that ladder connects earth with heaven, with Jesus Christ. A man can climb it, for the base rests upon the earth and the top-most round reaches into heaven....

Ye inhabitants of the earth, praise Him! And why? Because through Jesus Christ—whose long human arm encircles the race, while with His divine arm He grasps the throne of the Infinite—the gulf is bridged with His own body, and this atom of a world which was separated from the continent of heaven by sin and became an island is again reinstated, because Christ bridged the gulf (MS 5, 1891).

Chapter 31

50 Laban Understood the Wrong of Polygamy.—Laban understood the wrong of polygamy, although it was alone through his artifice that Jacob had taken two wives. He well knew that it was the jealousy of Leah and Rachel that led them to give their maids to Jacob, which confused the family relation, and increased the unhappiness of his daughters. And now as his daughters are journeying at a great distance from him, and their interest is to be entirely separate from his own, he would guard as far as possible their happiness. Laban would not have Jacob bring still greater unhappiness upon himself and upon Leah and Rachel, by taking other wives (Spiritual Gifts 3:126).

Chapter 32

24 Victory Sure When Self Is Surrendered.—Jacob "had power over the angel, and prevailed." Through humiliation, repentance, and self-surrender this sinful, erring mortal prevailed with the Majesty of heaven. He has fastened his trembling grasp on the promises of God, and the heart of infinite love could not turn away the sinner's plea. ...

Let no one despair of gaining the victory. Victory is sure when self is surrendered to God (MS 2, 1903).

26 (Matthew 11:12). **Determined Effort and Faith Essential.**—Jacob was in fear and distress while he sought in his own strength to obtain the victory. He mistook the divine visitor for an enemy, and contended with him while he had any strength left. But when he cast himself upon the mercy of God, he found that instead of being in the hands of an enemy, he was encircled in the arms of infinite love. He saw God face to face, and his sins were pardoned. "The kingdom of heaven suffereth violence, and the violent take it by force." This violence takes in the whole heart. To be double minded is to be unstable. Resolution, self-denial and consecrated effort are required for the work of preparation. The understanding and the conscience may be united; but if the will is not set to work, we shall make a failure. Every faculty and feeling must be engaged. Ardor and earnest prayer must take the place of listlessness and indifference. Only by earnest, determined effort and faith in the merits of Christ can we overcome, and gain the kingdom of heaven. Our time for work is short. Christ is soon to come the second time (The Youth's Instructor, May 24, 1900).

Chapter 35

2, 3 Jacob's Efforts to Remove Wrong Accepted.—Jacob was humbled, and required his family to humble themselves, and to lay off all their ornaments, for he was to make an atonement for their sins, by offering a sacrifice unto God, that He might be entreated for them, and not leave them to be destroyed by other nations. God accepted the efforts of Jacob to remove the wrong from his family, and appeared unto him, and blessed him, and renewed the promise made to him, because His fear was before him (Spiritual Gifts 3:137).

Chapter 37

4 Joseph Illustrates Christ.—Joseph illustrates Christ. Jesus came to His own, but His own received Him not. He was rejected and despised, because His acts were righteous, and His consistent, self-denying life was a continual rebuke upon those who professed piety, but whose lives were corrupt. Joseph's integrity and virtue were fiercely assailed, and she who would lead him astray could not prevail, therefore her hatred was strong against the virtue and integrity which she could not corrupt, and she testified falsely against him. The innocent suffered because of his righteousness. He was cast into prison because of his virtue. Joseph was sold to his enemies by his own brethren for a small sum of money. The Son of God was sold to His bitterest enemies by one of His own disciples. Jesus was meek and holy. His was a life of unexampled self-denial, goodness, and holiness. He was not guilty of any wrong. Yet false witnesses were hired to testify against Him. He was hated because He had been a faithful reprover of sin and corruption. Joseph's brethren stripped him of his coat of many colors. The executioners of Jesus cast lots for His seamless coat (Spiritual Gifts 3:174).

17-20 Joseph Shrank From Presence of His Brothers.—His [Joseph's] brothers rudely repulsed him. He told them his errand, but they answered him not. Joseph was alarmed at their angry looks. Fear took the place of joy, and he instinctively shrank with dread from their presence. They then took hold of him violently. They taunted him with the admonitions he had given them in the past, accused him of relating his dreams to exalt himself above them in the mind of their father, that he might love him more than themselves (Spiritual Gifts 3:140).

28, 36 Joseph Brought Blessing to Egypt.—Joseph regarded his being sold into Egypt as the greatest calamity that could have befallen him; but he saw the necessity of trusting in God as he had never done when protected by his father's love. Joseph brought God with him into Egypt, and the fact was made apparent by his cheerful demeanor amid his sorrow. As the ark of God brought rest and prosperity to Israel, so did this God-loving, God-fearing youth bring a blessing to Egypt. This was manifested in so marked a manner that Potiphar, in whose house he served, attributed all his blessings to his purchased slave, and made him a son rather than a servant. It is God's purpose that those who love and honor His name shall be honored also themselves, and that the glory given to

God through them shall be reflected upon themselves (The Youth's Instructor, March 11, 1897).

Chapter 39

9 Early Impressions Fortified Heart.—The early impressions made upon his [Joseph's] mind garrisoned his heart in the hour of fierce temptation, and led him to exclaim, "How can I do this great wickedness, and sin against God?" Childhood is the season in which the most abiding impressions may be made....

The seeds sown in infancy by the careful, God-fearing mother will become trees of righteousness, which will blossom and bear fruit; and the lessons given by a God-fearing father by precept and example, will, as in the case of Joseph, yield an abundant harvest by-and-by (HR 1880).

Entire Future Suspended on Moment's Decision.—Few temptations are more dangerous or more fatal to young men than the temptation to sensuality and none if yielded to will prove so decidedly ruinous to soul and body for time and eternity. The welfare of his entire future is suspended upon the decision of a moment. Joseph calmly casts his eyes to heaven for help, slips off his loose outer garment, leaving it in the hand of his tempter and while his eye is lighted with determined resolve in the place of unholy passion, he exclaims, "How can I do this great wickedness, and sin against God?" The victory is gained; he flees from the enchanter; he is saved (Letter 3, 1879).

9-19 Providence Will Overrule Enemy's Devices.—Amidst the snares to which all are exposed, they need strong and trustworthy defenses on which to rely. Many in this corrupt age have so small a supply of the grace of God, that in many instances their defense is broken down by the first assault, and fierce temptations take them captives. The shield of grace can preserve all unconquered by the temptations of the enemy, though surrounded with the most corrupting influences. By firm principle, and unwavering trust in God, their virtue and nobleness of character can shine, and, although surrounded with evil, no taint need be left upon their virtue and integrity. And if like Joseph they suffer calumny and false accusations, Providence will overrule all the enemy's devices for good, and God will in His own time exalt as much higher, as for a while they were debased by wicked revenge (Spiritual Gifts 3:145, 146).

20 (Lamentations 3:27; Matthew 23:12). Seeming Prosperity of Vice, a Severe Test.—Joseph's faithful integrity led to the loss of his reputation and his liberty. This is the severest test that the virtuous and God-fearing are subjected to, that vice seems to prosper while virtue is trampled in the dust. The seducer was living in prosperity as a model of virtuous propriety, while Joseph, true to principle, was under a degrading charge of crime the most revolting. Joseph's religion kept his temper sweet and his sympathy with humanity warm and strong, notwithstanding all his trials. There are those who if they feel they are not rightly used, become sour, ungenerous, crabbed and uncourteous in their words and deportment. They sink down discouraged, hateful and hating others. But Joseph was a Christian. No sooner does he enter upon prison life, than he brings all the brightness of his Christian principles into active exercise; he begins to make himself useful to others. He enters into the troubles of his fellow prisoners. He is cheerful, for he is a Christian gentleman. God was preparing him under this discipline for a situation of great responsibility, honor, and usefulness, and he was willing to learn; he took kindly to the lessons the Lord would teach him. He learned to bear the yoke in his youth. He learned to govern by first learning obedience himself. He humbled himself, and the Lord exalted him to special honor (Letter 3, 1879).

Hardships Prepared Joseph for Exalted Position.—The part which Joseph acted in connection with the scenes of the gloomy prison, was that which raised him finally to prosperity and honor. God designed that he should obtain an experience by temptations, adversity, and hardships, to prepare him to fill an exalted position (Spiritual Gifts 3:146).

Chapter 41

38-40 Secret of Fidelity.—Joseph carried his religion everywhere, and this was the secret of his unwavering fidelity (MS 59, 1897).

38 Men Recognize a Living Connection With God.—He who receives Christ by living faith has a living connection with God, and is a vessel unto honor. He carries with him the atmosphere of heaven, which is the grace of God, a treasure that the world cannot buy. He who is in living connection with God may be in humble stations, yet his moral worth is as precious as was that of Joseph and Daniel, who were recognized by heathen kings as men with whom was the Spirit of God (MS 54, 1894).

Chapter 42

21 Joseph's Brothers Feared Slavery.—They [Joseph's brothers] sold Joseph as a slave, and they were fearful that God designed to punish them by suffering them to become slaves (Spiritual Gifts 3:156).

Chapter 45

5 Minds of Brothers Relieved.—They [Joseph's brothers] humbly confessed their wrongs which they had committed against Joseph, and entreated his forgiveness, and were greatly rejoiced to find that he was alive; for they had suffered remorse, and great distress of mind, since their cruelty toward him. And now as they knew that they were not guilty of his blood, their troubled minds were relieved (Spiritual Gifts 3:167).

Chapter 49

3, 4 (Ch. 39.9). Unstable as Water.—There are those to be met with everywhere who have no fixed principles. It is hard for them to resist temptation. Let it come from what quarter, and in what form it may, and every precaution must be taken to surround them with influences that will strengthen their moral power. Let them be separated from these helpful influences and association, be thrown with a class who are irreligious, and they will soon show that they have no real hold from above; they trusted in their own strength. They have been praised and exalted when their feet were standing in sliding sand. They are like Reuben, unstable as water, having no inward rectitude, and like Reuben they will never excel. What you need is to see your dependence upon God, and to have a resolute heart. Be a man where you are; show strength of character where you are; be able, through Jesus Christ, to say, "No, I will not do this great wickedness, and sin against God." That kind of easy good nature which can never nerve itself to give decided refusal to any proposal that would injure his moral and religious influence in the sight of God and of man is always under the control of Satan far more than under the control of the Spirit of God. They are led into evil very easily because they have a very accommodating disposition, and it hurts them to give a square No, "I will not do this wickedness and sin against God." If invited to take a glass with merry men or women, they are led as an ox to the slaughter, they join with the impious, who laugh at the ready compliance afterwards. There is no interior strength to fall back upon. They do not make God their trust. They have no high principles of duty (Letter 48, 1887).

Exodus

Chapter 1

1 See EGW comment on Deuteronomy 1:1.

8 Egyptians Sinned in Refusing Light.—The sin of the Egyptians was that they had refused the light which God had so graciously sent to them through Joseph (The Youth's Instructor, April 15, 1897).

Chapter 2

10 (Hebrews 11:26, 27). In Egypt Moses Studied Laws of God.—The strength of Moses was his connection with the Source of all power, the Lord God of hosts. He rises grandly above every earthly inducement, and trusts himself wholly to God. He considered that he was the Lord's. While he was connected with the official interests of the king of Egypt, he was constantly studying the laws of God's government, and thus his faith grew. That faith was of value to him. It was deeply rooted in the soil of his earliest teachings, and the culture of his life was to prepare him for the great work of delivering Israel from bondage. He meditated on these things; he was constantly listening to his commission from God. After slaying the Egyptian, he saw that he had not understood God's plan, and he fled from Egypt and became a shepherd. He was no longer planning to do a great work, but he became very humble; the mists that were beclouding his mind were expelled, and he disciplined his mind to seek after God as his refuge (Letter 21a, 1893).

11 (Acts 7:22). Training for Two Generalships.—Moses was a man of intelligence. In the providence of God he was given opportunity to gain a fitness for a great work. He was thoroughly educated as a general. When he went out to meet the enemy, he was successful; and on his return from battle, his praises were sung by the whole army. Notwithstanding this, he constantly remembered that through him God purposed to deliver the children of Israel (The Youth's Instructor, January 29, 1903).

Chapter 3

1 Jethro Singled Out.—Jethro was singled out from the darkness of the Gentile world to reveal the principles of heaven. God has ever had appointed agencies, and has ever given abundant evidences that these agencies were heaven-appointed and heaven-sent (Letter 190, 1905).

Moses Transferred to a Private School.—God transferred Moses from the courts of luxury, where his every wish was gratified, to a more private school. Here the Lord could commune with Moses and so educate him that he would obtain a knowledge of the hardships, trials, and perils of the wilderness (The Youth's Instructor, December 13, 1900).

2-5 Burning Bush a Reality.—It will baffle the keenest intellect to interpret the divine manifestation of the burning bush. It was not a dream; it was not a vision; it was a living reality,—something that Moses saw with his eyes. He heard the voice of God calling to him out of the bush, and he covered his face, realizing that he stood in the immediate presence of God. God was conversing with humanity. Never could Moses describe the impression made upon his mind by the sight he then saw, and by the sound of the voice that spoke to him; but this impression was never effaced. Heaven came very near to him as, with reverent awe, he listened to the words, "I am the God of thy father, the God of Abraham, the God of Isaac, and the God of Jacob." What wondrous condescension for God to leave the heavenly courts, and manifest Himself to Moses, talking with him face to face, "as a man speaketh unto his friend" (The Youth's Instructor, December 20, 1900).

14 God Sees Future as We See Present.—I Am means an eternal presence; the past, present, and future are alike to God. He sees the most remote events of past history, and the far distant future with as clear a vision as we do those things that are transpiring daily. We know not what is before us, and if we did, it would not contribute to our eternal welfare. God gives us an opportunity to exercise faith and trust in the great I AM (Lt 119, 1895).

20 Plagues a Sign of God's Power Over All.—When the children of Israel were in bondage to the Egyptians, God revealed Himself as a God above all human authority, all human greatness. The signs and miracles He wrought in behalf of His people show His power over nature, and over the greatest among those who worshiped nature, who ignored the power that made nature.

God went through the proud land of Egypt just as He will go through the earth in the last days (The Review and Herald, July 10, 1900).

Chapter 4

10 Fearful of Bringing Self Into Work.—When, after Moses' time of preparation and trial was over, he was once more told to go and deliver Israel, he was self-distrustful, slow of speech, timid. "Who am I," he said, "that I should go unto Pharaoh, and that I should bring forth the children of Israel out of Egypt?" He pleaded as an excuse a lack of ready speech. He had been the general of the armies of Egypt, and he certainly knew how to speak. But he was afraid that he would bring self into his work (MS 11, 1903).

21 Rejection of Light Hardens Heart.—Pharaoh saw the mighty working of the Spirit of God; he saw the miracles which the Lord performed by His servant; but he refused obedience to God's command. The rebellious king had proudly inquired, "Who is the Lord, that I should obey his voice to let Israel go? ...[Exodus 5:2]." And as the judgments of God fell more and more heavily upon him, he persisted in stubborn resistance. By rejecting light from heaven, he became hard and unimpressible. The providence of God was revealing His power, and these manifestations, unacknowledged, were the means of hardening Pharaoh's heart against greater light. Those who exalt their own ideas above the plainly specified will of God, are saying as did Pharaoh, "Who is the Lord, that I should obey His voice?" Every rejection of light hardens the heart and darkens the understanding; and thus men find it more and more difficult to distinguish between right and wrong, and they become bolder in resisting the will of God (MS 3, 1885).

(Matthew 12:31, 32). God Gave Pharaoh Into Hands of Self.—Every additional evidence of the power of God that the Egyptian monarch resisted, carried him on to a stronger and more persistent defiance of God. Thus the work went on, finite man warring against the expressed will of an infinite God. This case is a clear illustration of the sin against the Holy Ghost. "Whatsoever a man soweth, that shall he also reap." Gradually the Lord withdrew His Spirit. Removing His restraining power, He gave the king into the hands of the worst of all tyrants,—self (The Review and Herald, July 27, 1897).

(Galatians 6:7). Pharaoh Sowed Obstinacy, Reaped Obstinacy.— "Whatsoever a man soweth, that shall he also reap." Pharaoh sowed obstinacy, and he reaped obstinacy. He himself put this seed into the soil. There was no more need for God by some new power to interfere with its growth, than there is for Him to interfere with the growth of a grain of corn. All that is required is that a seed shall be left to germinate and spring up to bring forth fruit after its kind. The harvest reveals the kind of seed that has been sown (MS 126, 1901).

Rebellion Produces Rebellion.—After the plague was stayed, the king refused to let Israel go. Rebellion produces rebellion. The king had become so hardened with his continual opposition to the will of God, that his whole being rose in rebellion to the awful exhibitions of His divine power (Spiritual Gifts 3:215).

Israel Would Be Preserved, Even if Pharaoh Had to Die.—Pharaoh hardened his heart against the Lord and he ventured, notwithstanding all the signs and mighty wonders he had witnessed, to threaten that if Moses and Aaron appeared before him again they should die. If the king had not become hardened in his rebellion against God, he would have been humbled under a sense of the power of the living God who could save or destroy. He would have known that He who could do such miracles, and multiply His signs and wonders, would preserve the lives of His chosen servants, even if He should have to slay the king of Egypt (Spiritual Gifts 3:220).

Chapter 7

10-12 Magicians' Work a Counterfeit.—The magicians seemed to perform several things with their enchantments similar to those things which God wrought by the hand of Moses and Aaron. They did not really cause their rods to become serpents, but by magic, aided by the great deceiver, made them to appear like serpents, to counterfeit the work of God. Satan assisted his servants to resist the work of the Most High, in order to deceive the people, and encourage them in their rebellion. Pharaoh would grasp at the least evidence he could obtain to justify himself in resisting the work of God, performed by Moses and Aaron. He told these servants of God that his magicians could do all these wonders. The difference between the work of God and that of the magicians was, one was of God, and the other of Satan. One was true, the other false (Spiritual Gifts 3:205, 206).

Chapter 8

7 Pharaoh Continued Devotions During Plagues.—During the plagues on Egypt Pharaoh was punctual in his superstitious devotion to the river, and visited it every morning, and as he stood upon its banks he offered praise and thanksgiving to the water, recounting the great good it accomplished, and telling the water of its great power; that without it they could not exist; for their lands were watered by it, and it supplied meat for their tables (4SG 54, 55).

Chapter 9

3 Effect of Plagues Tested.—Those who regarded the word of the Lord gathered their cattle into barns and houses, while those whose hearts were hardened, like Pharaoh's, left their cattle in the field. Here was an opportunity to test the exalted pride of the Egyptians, and to show the number whose hearts were really affected by the wonderful dealings of God with His people, whom they had despised and cruelly entreated (Spiritual Gifts 3:214).

Chapter 11

1, 8 Moses Fearlessly Met Pharaoh Again.—Notwithstanding Moses had been forbidden to come again into the presence of Pharaoh, for in the day he should see his face he should die, yet he had one more message from God for the rebellious king, and he firmly walked into his presence, and stood fearlessly before him to declare to him the word of the Lord....

As Moses told the king of the plague which would come upon them, more dreadful than any had yet visited Egypt, which would cause all his great counselors to bow down before him, and entreat the Israelites to leave Egypt, the king was exceedingly angry. He was enraged because he could not intimidate Moses, and make him tremble before his kingly authority. But Moses leaned for support upon a mightier arm than that of any earthly monarch (Spiritual Gifts 3:221, 222).

Chapter 12

31, 32 Pharaoh Brought From Pride to Humility.—When the Egyptians, from the king upon his throne down to the lowliest servant, were afflicted, and their firstborn were slain, then there was wailing throughout all Egypt. Then

Pharaoh remembered his proud boast, "Who is the Lord that I should obey his voice, to let Israel go? I know not the Lord, neither will I let Israel go." He humbled himself and went with his counselors and his rulers to Goshen in haste, and bowed before Moses and Aaron, and bid them go and serve their God. Their flocks and herds should go also as they had requested. They implored them to be gone, fearing if they continued longer, they would be all as dead men. Pharaoh also entreated Moses to bless him, thinking at the time that a blessing from the servant of God would protect him from the further effects of the dreadful plague (Spiritual Gifts 3:246).

38 Many Egyptians Acknowledged God.—There was quite a large number of the Egyptians who were led to acknowledge, by manifestations of the signs and wonders shown in Egypt, that the God of the Hebrews was the only true God. They entreated to be permitted to come to the houses of the Israelites with their families, upon that fearful night when the angel of God should slay the firstborn of the Egyptians. They were convinced that their gods whom they had worshiped were without knowledge, and had no power to save or to destroy. And they pledged themselves to henceforth choose the God of Israel as their God. They decided to leave Egypt, and go with the children of Israel to worship their God. The Israelites welcomed the believing Egyptians to their houses (Spiritual Gifts 3:224, 225).

Chapter 14

15, 16, 21, 22 Hand of Christ Rolled Back Waters.—The mighty hand of Christ rolled back the waters of the Red Sea, so that they stood up like a wall. Thus He made a dry passage through the sea, and Israel passed over dryshod (MS 155, 1899).

23, 26-28 Pursuit of Israel Closed Egyptians' Probation.—When the whole army,—"all Pharaoh's horses, his chariots, and his horsemen,"—were in the very bed of the sea, the Lord said unto Moses, "Stretch out thy rod over the sea." Israel had passed over on dry land, but they heard the shouting of he armies in pursuit. As Moses stretched out his rod over the sea, the embanked waters that had stood as a great wall, rolled on in their natural course. Of all the men of Egypt in that vast army, not one escaped. All perished in their determination to have their own way and to refuse God's way. That occasion was the end of their probation (MS 35, 1906).

25-27 Pharaoh Perished in Red Sea.—The monarch hardened his heart, and went on from one step to another of unbelief, until throughout the vast realm of Egypt the firstborn, the pride of every household, had been laid low. After this he hurried with his army after Israel. He sought to bring back a people delivered by the arm of Omnipotence. But he was fighting against a Power greater than any human power, and with his host he perished in the waters of the Red Sea (MS 126, 1901).

Chapter 15

23-25 (Jeremiah 8:22) A Balm for Every Wound.—When Moses presented before the Lord the sad difficulties of the children of Israel, He did not present some new remedy, but called their attention to that which was at hand; for there was a bush or shrub which He had created that was to be cast into the water to make the fountain sweet and pure. When this was done, the suffering people could drink of the water with safety and pleasure. God has provided a balm for every wound. There is a balm in Gilead, there is a physician there (Letter 65a, 1894).

Chapter 16

3 (1 Corinthians 6:20). Effects of Appetite in Israel's Experience.—Whenever their appetite was restricted, the Israelites were dissatisfied, and murmured and complained against Moses and Aaron, and against God.... But God was proving His people. In order to develop what was in their hearts, He allowed them to pass through severe trials. When they failed, He brought them around to the same point again, trying them a little more closely and severely

In Egypt their taste had become perverted. God designed to restore their appetite to a pure, healthy state, in order that they might enjoy the simple fruits that were given to Adam and Eve in Eden. He was about to establish them in a second Eden, a goodly land, where they might enjoy the fruits and grains that He would provide for them. He purposed to remove the feverish diet upon which they had subsisted in Egypt; for He wished them to be in perfect health and soundness when they entered the goodly land to which He was leading them, so that the surrounding heathen nations might be constrained to glorify the God of Israel, the God who had done so wonderful a work for His people. Unless the people who acknowledged Him as the God of heaven were in perfect soundness of health, His name could not be glorified.

If the Israelites had submitted to God's requirements, they would have had a healthy posterity. But they chose to follow their own way, walking after the imagination of their own hearts. They gratified their appetites and consulted their own tastes and wishes. As a result, the wilderness was strewn with their dead bodies. Of all the vast multitude that left Egypt, six hundred thousand mighty men of war, besides women and children, only two entered the promised land (MS 69, 1912).

10 Cost of Disobedience.—If all the teachings given by Christ when enshrouded in the pillar of cloud, had been obeyed, the Jewish nation would have stood forth to glorify God above every nation and people upon the face of the earth. Jerusalem need not have been destroyed. But she disregarded the commandments of God, while professedly regarding them (Letter 195, 1899).

14, 15 Wilderness Diet Made Israel More Manageable.—If the Israelites had been given the diet to which they had been accustomed while in Egypt, they would have exhibited the unmanageable spirit that the world is exhibiting today. In the diet of men and women in this age there are included many things that the Lord would not have permitted the children of Israel to eat. The human family as it is today is an illustration of what the children of Israel would have been if God had allowed them to eat the food and follow the habits and customs of the Egyptians (Letter 44, 1903).

29 (Ch. 20:8-11). Miracle Preserved Sabbath.—By a miracle God preserved the Sabbath law through the forty years of wilderness wandering (MS 77, 1899).

Chapter 17

14-16 (1 Samuel 15:2, 3). Amalek Doomed to Destruction.—Many years before, God had appointed Amalek to utter destruction. They had lifted up their hands against God, and His throne, and had taken oath by their gods that Israel should be utterly consumed, and the God of Israel brought down so that He would not be able to deliver them out of their hands.

Amalek had made derision of the fears of his people, and made sport of God's wonderful works for the deliverance of Israel performed by the hand of Moses before the Egyptians. They had boasted that their wise men and magicians could perform all those wonders. And if the children of Israel had been their captives, in their power as they were in Pharaoh's, that the God of Israel Himself would not have been able to deliver them out of their hands. They despised Israel, and vowed to plague them until there should not be one left (4SG 72, 73).

God did not wish His people to possess anything which belonged to the Amalekites, for His curse rested upon them and their possessions. He designed that they should have an end, and that His people should not preserve anything for themselves which He had cursed. He also wished the nations to see the end of that people who had defied Him, and to mark that they were destroyed by the very people they had despised. They were not to destroy them to add to their own possessions, or to get glory to themselves, but to fulfill the word of the Lord spoken in regard to Amalek (Spiritual Gifts 3:75).

Chapter 18

13 See EGW comment on Numbers 12:3.

Chapter 19

3 Ancient Instruction to Be Studied.—The instructions given to Moses for ancient Israel, with their sharp, rigid outlines, are to be studied and obeyed by the people of God today (Letter 259, 1903).

Moses and God in Secret Council.—Moses, the visible leader of the Israelites, was admitted into the secret councils of the Most High. The people were given evidence that Moses did indeed talk with God, receiving from Him the instruction given them ((Ibid.).

3-8 God's Covenant Our Refuge.—The covenant that God made with His people at Sinai is to be our refuge and defense. The Lord said to Moses:—

"Thus shalt thou say to the house of Jacob, and tell the children of Israel: Ye have seen what I did unto the Egyptians, and how I bare you on eagles' wings, and brought you unto myself. Now therefore, if ye will obey my voice indeed, and keep my covenant, than ye shall be a peculiar treasure unto me above all people: for all the earth is mine: and ye shall be unto me a kingdom of priests, and an holy nation."

"And Moses came and called for the elders of the people, and laid before their faces all these words."

"And all the people answered together, and said, All that the Lord hath spoken we will do."

This covenant is of just as much force today as it was when the Lord made it with ancient Israel (The Southern Work, March 1, 1904).

7, 8 (quoted) (Isaiah 56:5). A Pledge to the Covenant.—This is the pledge that God's people are to make in these last days. Their acceptance with God depends on a faithful fulfilment of the terms of their agreement with Him. God includes in His covenant all who will obey Him. To all who will do justice and judgment, keeping their hand from doing any evil, the promise is, "Even unto them will I give in mine house and within my walls a place and a name better than of sons and of daughters: I will give them an everlasting name, that shall not be cut off" (The Review and Herald, June 23, 1904).

9 Glory of Cloud Emanated From Christ.—The cloud that guided Israel, stood over the tabernacle. The glory of the cloud emanated from Jesus Christ, who from the midst of the glory talked with Moses, as He had talked with him from the burning bush. The brightness of God's presence was enshrouded in the darkness of the cloud which He made His pavilion, that the people could endure to look upon the cloud, as seeing Him who is invisible. This was God's plan whereby He might approach man (MS 126, 1901).

Chapter 20

1-17 (Nehemiah 9:6-15). Father by Side of Son in Giving Law.—When the law was spoken, the Lord, the Creator of heaven and earth, stood by the side of His Son, enshrouded in the fire and the smoke on the mount. It was not here that the law was first given; but it was proclaimed, that the children of Israel, whose ideas had become confused in their association with idolaters in Egypt, might be reminded of its terms, and understand what constitutes the true worship of Jehovah (The Signs of the Times, October 15, 1896).

Adam and Eve Knew the Law.—Adam and Eve, at their creation, had a knowledge of the law of God. It was printed on their hearts, and they understood its claims upon them (MS 99, 1902).

The law of God existed before man was created. It was adapted to the condition of holy beings; even angels were governed by it. After the fall, the principles of righteousness were unchanged. Nothing was taken from the law;

not one of its holy precepts could be improved. And as it has existed from the beginning, so will it continue to exist throughout the ceaseless ages of eternity. "Concerning thy testimonies," says the psalmist, "I have known of old that thou hast founded them forever (The Signs of the Times, April 15, 1886).

Law Suited to Holy Order of Beings.—The Sabbath of the fourth commandment was instituted in Eden. After God had made the world, and created man upon the earth, He made the Sabbath for man. After Adam's sin and fall nothing was taken from the law of God. The principles of the ten commandments existed before the fall, and were of a character suited to the condition of a holy order of beings. After the fall, the principles of those precepts were not changed, but additional precepts were given to meet man in his fallen state (Spiritual Gifts 3:295).

Worded to Meet Fallen Intelligences.—The law of Jehovah dating back to creation, was comprised in the two great principles, "Thou shalt love the Lord thy God with all thy heart, and with all thy soul, and with all thy mind, and with all thy strength. This is the first commandment. And the second is like, namely this: Thou shalt love thy neighbor as thyself. There is none other commandment greater than these." These two great principles embrace the first four commandments, showing the duty of man to God, and the last six, showing the duty of man to his fellowman. The principles were more explicitly stated to man after the fall, and worded to meet the case of fallen intelligences. This was necessary in consequence of the minds of men being blinded by transgression (The Signs of the Times, April 15, 1875 [Reprinted in RH May 6, 1875]).

The law of God existed before the creation of man or else Adam could not have sinned. After the transgression of Adam the principles of the law were not changed, but were definitely arranged and expressed to meet man in his fallen condition. Christ, in counsel with His Father, instituted the system of sacrificial offerings; that death, instead of being immediately visited upon the transgressor, should be transferred to a victim which should prefigure the great and perfect offering of the son of God (The Signs of the Times, March 14, 1878).

Precepts Given to Guard Decalogue.—In consequence of continual transgression, the moral law was repeated in awful grandeur from Sinai. Christ gave to Moses religious precepts which were to govern everyday life. These statutes were explicitly given to guard the ten commandments. They were not shadowy types to pass away with the death of Christ. They were to be binding upon men in every age as long as time should last. These commands were enforced by the power of the moral law, and they clearly and definitely explained that law (The Signs of the Times, April 15, 1875 [Reprinted in The Review and Herald, May 6, 1875]).

(Isaiah 58:13, 14). Every Specification Is God's Character.—The God of heaven has placed a benediction upon them that keep the commandments of God. Shall we stand as a peculiar people of God, or shall we trample upon the law of God and say it is not binding? God might just as well have abolished Himself. In the law every specification is the character of the infinite God (MS 12, 1894).

Law Denounces Slightest Sin.—God has given His law for the regulation of the conduct of nations, of families, and of individuals. There is not one worker of wickedness, though his act be the lightest and the most secret, that escapes the denunciation of that law (MS 58, 1897).

Holiness Made Known.—Our duty to obey this law is to be the burden of this last message of mercy to the world. God's law is not a new thing. It is not holiness created, but holiness made known. It is a code of principles expressing mercy, goodness, and love. It presents to fallen humanity the character of God, and states plainly the whole duty of man (MS 88, 1897).

(John 14:15). Ten Commandments—Ten Promises.—The ten commandments, Thou shalt, and Thou shalt not, are ten promises, assured to us if we render obedience to the law governing the universe. "If ye love me, keep my commandments." Here is the sum and substance of the law of God. The terms of salvation for every son and daughter of Adam are here outlined (MS 41, 1896).

The ten holy precepts spoken by Christ upon Sinai's mount were the revelation of the character of God, and made known to the world the fact that He had jurisdiction over the whole human heritage. That law of ten precepts of the greatest love that can be presented to man is the voice of God from heaven speaking to the soul in promise, "This do, and you will not come under the dominion and control of Satan." There is not a negative in that law, although it may appear thus. It is DO, and Live (Letter 89, 1898).

(Romans 12:1; 2 Peter 1:4). A Wall of Protection.—In the ten commandments God has laid down the laws of His kingdom. Any violation of the laws of nature is a violation of the law of God.

The Lord has given His holy commandments to be a wall of protection around His created beings, and those who will keep themselves from the defilement of appetite and passion may become partakers of the divine nature. Their perceptions will be clear. They will know how to preserve every faculty in health, so that it may be presented to God in service. The Lord can use them: for they understand the words of the great apostle, "I beseech you, therefore, brethren, by the mercies of God, that ye present your bodies a living sacrifice, holy, acceptable unto God, which is your reasonable service" (MS 153, 1899).

3-17 (Proverbs 4:20-22). Health in Obedience to God's Law.—The love of Jesus in the soul will banish all hatred, selfishness, and envy; for the law of the Lord is perfect, converting the soul. There is health in obedience to God's law. The affections of the obedient are drawn out after God. Looking unto the Lord Jesus, we may encourage and serve one another. The love of Christ is shed abroad in our souls, and there is no dissension and strife among us (MS 152, 1901).

No Others Professed to Keep Commandments.—The ancient Jewish church were the highly favored people of God, brought out of Egypt and acknowledged as His own peculiar treasure. The many and exceeding great and precious promises to them as a people, were the hope and confidence of the Jewish church. Herein they trusted, and believed their salvation sure. No other people professed to be governed by the commandments of God (Redemption: or the First Advent of Christ, p. 35).

3 Self-dependence Is Idolatry.—Idolaters are condemned by the Word of God. Their folly consists in trusting in self for salvation, in bowing down to the works of their own hands. God classes as idolaters those who trust in their own wisdom, their own devising, depending for success on their riches and power, striving to strengthen themselves by alliance with men whom the world calls great, but who fail to discern the binding claims of His law (The Review and Herald, March 15, 1906).

False Conceptions of God Are Idolatry.—Are we worshipers of Jehovah, or of Baal? of the living God, or of idols? No outward shrines may be visible; there may be no image for the eye to rest upon; yet we may be practising idolatry. It is as easy to make an idol of cherished ideas or objects as to fashion gods of wood or stone. Thousands have a false conception of God and His attributes. They are as verily serving a false God as were the servants of Baal (The Review and Herald, December 3, 1908).

Satan Plants Throne Between Heaven and Earth.—Satan accomplished the fall of man, and since that time it has been his work to efface in man the image of God, and to stamp upon human hearts his own image. Possessing supremacy in guilt, he claims supremacy for himself, and exercises over his subjects the power of royalty. He cannot expel God from His throne, but through the system of idolatry, he plants his own throne between the heaven and the earth, between God and the human worshiper (The Review and Herald, October 22, 1895).

4-6 Second Commandment and Pictures.—A few condemned pictures, urging that they are prohibited by the second commandment, and that everything of this kind should be destroyed.... The second commandment prohibits image worship; but God himself employed pictures and symbols to represent to His prophets lessons which He would have them give to the people, and which could thus be better understood than if given in any other way. He appealed to the understanding through the sense of sight. Prophetic history was presented to Daniel and John in symbols, and these were to be represented plainly upon tables, that he who read might understand (Historical Sketches of the Foreign Missions of the Seventh-day Adventists, 212).

8-11 (Genesis 2:9, 16, 17; Exodus 16:29). Sabbath, a Test of Loyalty.—Every man has been placed on trial, as were Adam and Eve in Eden. As the tree of knowledge was placed in the midst of the garden of Eden, so the Sabbath command is placed in the midst of the decalogue. In regard to the fruit of the tree of knowledge, the restriction was made, "Ye shall not eat of it, ...lest ye die" [Genesis 3:3]. Of the Sabbath, God said, Ye shall not defile it, but keep it holy.... As the tree of knowledge was the test of Adam's obedience, so the fourth command is the test that God has given to prove the loyalty of all His people. The experience of Adam is to be a warning to us so long as time shall last. It warns us not to receive any assurance from the mouth of men or of angels that will detract one jot or tittle from the sacred law of Jehovah (The Review and Herald, August 30, 1898).

14 False Worship Is Spiritual Adultery.—All false worship is spiritual adultery. The second precept, which forbids false worship, is also a command to worship God, and Him only serve. The Lord is a jealous God. He will not Be trifled with. He has spoken concerning the manner in which He should be worshiped. He has a hatred of idolatry; for its influence is corrupting. It debases the mind, and leads to sensuality and all kinds of sin (MS 126, 1901).

16 (Galatians 6:7). Flippant Speech May Be False Witness.—Slander covers more ground than we suppose. The command, "Thou shalt not bear false witness," means very much more than we realize. False witness is borne again and again in flippant speech concerning even the workers whom God has sent. The seeds of envy, of evil thinking and evil speaking, germinate and produce a harvest of their kind, to be garnered by the one who planted the seed. "Whatsoever a man soweth, that shall he also reap" (Letter 9, 1892).

Chapter 21

1-6 Care of the Interests of Servants.—The Lord desired to guard the interests of servants. He commanded the Israelites to be merciful, and to bear in mind that they themselves had been servants. They were directed to be mindful of the rights of their servants. In no case were they to abuse them. In dealing with them they were not to be exacting, as the Egyptian taskmasters had been with them. They were to exercise tenderness and compassion in the treatment of their servants. God desired them to put themselves in the place of the servants, and deal with them as they would wish others to deal with them under the same circumstances.

Because of poverty, some were sold into bondage by their parents. Others who were sentenced for crimes by the judges were sold into bondage. The Lord specified that even these were not to be held as bond-servants for more than seven years. At the end of that time every servant was given his freedom, or, if he chose, he was allowed to remain with his master. Thus God guarded the interests of the lowly and the oppressed. Thus He enjoined a noble spirit of generosity, and encouraged all to cultivate a love for liberty, because the Lord had made them free. Any one who refused liberty when it was his privilege to have it, was marked. This was not a badge of honor to him, but a mark of disgrace. Thus God encouraged the cultivation of a high and noble spirit, rather than a spirit of bondage and slavery.

God desires Christians to respect the liberty that He has in so marvelous a manner given them. In Christ is vested the ownership of every man. Man should not be another man's property. God has bought mankind. One man's mind, one man's power, should not rule and control another's conscience. In the sight of God wealth and position do not exalt one man above another. Men are free to choose the service of God, to love the Lord, and to keep all His commandments (MS 126, 1901).

Chapter 23

16 (John 7). Christ's Sacrifice Provides Bounties.—The rivers of blood that flowed at the harvest thanksgiving, when the sacrifices were offered in such large numbers, were meant to teach a great truth. For even the productions of the earth, the bounties provided for man's sustenance, we are indebted to the offering of Christ upon the cross of Calvary. God teaches us that all we receive from Him is the gift of redeeming love (The Review and Herald, November 10, 1896).

Chapter 24

4-8 Ratification of the Covenant.—Preparation was now made for the ratification of the covenant, according to God's directions. ...

Here the people received the conditions of the covenant. They made a solemn covenant with God, typifying the covenant made between God and every believer in Jesus Christ. The conditions were plainly laid before the people. They were not left to misunderstand them. When they were requested to decide whether they would agree to all the conditions given, they unanimously consented to obey every obligation. They had already consented to obey God's commandments. The principles of the law were now particularized, that they might know how much was involved in covenanting to obey the law; and they accepted the specifically defined particulars of the law.

If the Israelites had obeyed God's requirements, they would have been practical Christians. They would have been happy; for they would have been keeping God's ways, and not following the inclinations of their own natural hearts. Moses did not leave them to misconstrue the words of the Lord or to misapply His requirements. He wrote all the words of the Lord in a book, that they might be referred to afterward. In the mount he had written them as Christ Himself dictated them.

Bravely did the Israelites speak the words promising obedience to the Lord, after hearing His covenant read in the audience of the people. They said, "All that the Lord hath said will we do, and be obedient." Then the people were set apart and sealed to God. A sacrifice was offered to the Lord. A portion of the blood of the sacrifice was sprinkled upon the altar. This signified that the people had consecrated themselves—body, mind, and soul—to God. A portion was sprinkled upon the people. This signified that through the sprinkled blood of Christ, God graciously accepted them as His special treasure. Thus the Israelites entered into a solemn covenant with God (MS 126, 1901).

Chapter 25

17-22 Living Angels Beside Heavenly Ark.—The ark of the earthly sanctuary was the pattern of the true ark in heaven. There, beside the heavenly ark, stand living angels, each with one wing overshadowing the mercy-seat, and stretching forth on high, while the other wings are folded over their forms in token of reverence and humility (The Signs of the Times, March 21, 1911).

Chapter 26

31 Temple Vail Renewed Yearly.—At the moment in which Christ died, there were priests ministering in the temple before the vail which separated the holy from the most holy place. Suddenly they felt the earth tremble beneath them, and the vail of the temple, a strong, rich drapery that had been renewed yearly, was rent in twain from top to bottom by the same bloodless hand that wrote the words of doom upon the walls of Belshazzar's palace (The Spirit of Prophecy 3:166, 167).

Chapter 27

1 (Ch. 38:1). Service of Altar Restored.—Directions were given for building an altar for the offering of sacrifices, a service which had been almost wholly discontinued. While in Egyptian bondage the people's ideas of sacrifice had been largely molded by the ideas of the Egyptians who had themselves learned from Israel when they first went into Egypt, but who had mingled with truth the falsehood of idolatry. They had most indecent practices in connection with the worship at their heathen altars. The law given in Eden and repeated on Sinai was essential for the Israel of God; for during the bondage in Egypt the claims of God and His commandments had been lost sight of. This is why the Lord uttered His holy law with an audible voice in the hearing of all the people. He desired that they should hear His commandments and obey them (MS 58, 1900).

Chapter 31

1-6 (1 Timothy 5:13). Meddling Punished by Death.—The Lord loves to see His work done as perfectly as possible. In the wilderness, the Israelites had to learn to accomplish with exactness and promptness the work connected with the order of the camp and especially the work of the tabernacle, its ornaments, and its service. All had to learn before they could accomplish this, to them new work. They had to be trained before they could do it as God desired. There were men there ready to give counsel and advice and to meddle with the work of mounting and dismounting the tabernacle; and those who neglected their special work to meddle with the work of others, thinking they had special wisdom and knew how it should be done, were put to death. Each one had to be taught the value of promptness and exactness in every position of trust. The memory had to be taxed, and they had to realize the responsibility of doing everything in due time.

This is the discipline which the Lord anciently gave to His people, and it is the discipline which should exist in our missions, our colleges, our publishing houses, our sanitariums. God likes to see men understand their weak points, and instead of closing their eyes to their defects, they should make persevering efforts to overcome them (MS 24, 1887).

How Could the Work Be Done?—Israel had been held all their days in the bondage of Egypt, and although there were ingenious men among them, they had not been instructed in the curious arts which were called for in the building of the tabernacle. They knew how to make bricks, but they did not understand how to work in gold and silver. How was the work to be done? Who was sufficient for these things? These were questions that troubled the mind of Moses.

Then God Himself explained how the work was to be accomplished. He signified by name the persons He desired to do a certain work. Bezaleel was to be the architect. This man belonged to the tribe of Judah,—a tribe that God delighted to honor (MS 29, 1908).

2-7. Did Not Depend on Skilled Egyptians.—In ancient times, the Lord instructed Moses to build Him a sanctuary. The people were to provide the material, and skillful men must be found to handle the precious material. Among the multitude were Egyptians, who had acted as overseers for such work, and thoroughly understood how it should be done. But the work was not dependent upon them. The Lord united with human agencies, giving them wisdom to work skillfully. [Exodus 31:2-7 quoted.]

Let the workmen in the service of God today pray to Him for wisdom and keen foresight, that they may do their work perfectly (MS 52, 1903).

13 (Ch. 25:8). Sabbath Kept During Construction.—God directed that a tabernacle should be built, where the Israelites, during their wilderness-journeying, could worship Him. Orders from heaven were given that this tabernacle should be built without delay. Because of the sacredness of the work and the need for haste, some argued that the work of the tabernacle should be carried forward on the Sabbath, as well as on the other days of the week. Christ heard these suggestions, and saw that the people were in great danger of being ensnared by concluding that they would be justified in working on the Sabbath that the tabernacle might be completed as quickly as possible. The word came to them, "Verily my Sabbaths ye shall keep." Though the work on the tabernacle must be carried forward with expedition, the Sabbath must not be employed as a working day. Even the work on the Lord's house must give way to the sacred observance of the Lord's rest day. Thus jealous is God for the honor of His memorial of creation (The Review and Herald, October 28, 1902).

18. Original Law in Heavenly Ark.—I warn you, Do not place your influence against God's commandments. That law is just as Jehovah wrote it in the temple of heaven. Man may trample upon its copy here below, but the original is kept in the ark of God in heaven; and on the cover of this ark, right above that law, is the mercy seat. Jesus stands right there before that ark to mediate for man (MS 6a, 1886).

Law Preserved in Ark.—"And He [Christ] gave unto Moses, when He had made an end of communicating with him upon Mount Sinai, two tables of testimony, tables of stone, written by the finger of God." Nothing written on those tables could be blotted out. The precious record of the law was placed in the ark of the testament and is still there, safely hidden from the human family. But in God's appointed time He will bring forth these tables of stone to be a testimony to all the world against the disregard of His commandments and against the idolatrous worship of a counterfeit Sabbath (MS 122, 1901).

There are abundant evidences of the immutability of God's law. It was written with the finger of God, never to be obliterated, never to be destroyed. The tables of stone are hidden by God, to be produced in the great judgment-day, just as He wrote them (The Review and Herald, March 26, 1908).

When the judgment shall sit, and the books shall be opened, and every man shall be judged according to the things written in the books, then the tables of stone, hidden by God until that day, will be presented before the world as the standard of righteousness. Then men and women will see that the prerequisite of their salvation is obedience to the perfect law of God. None will find excuse for sin. By the righteous principles of that law, men will receive their sentence of life or of death (The Review and Herald, January 28, 1909).

Chapter 32

1, 2 Aaron's Sin, Pacifying.—We repeat the sin of Aaron, pacifying, when the eyesight should be clear to discern evil and state it plainly, even if it places us in an unpleasant position, because our motives may be misapprehended. We must not suffer wrong upon a brother or any soul with whom we are connected. This neglect to stand up firmly for truth was the sin of Aaron. Had he spoken the truth plainly, that golden calf would never have been made. The same spirit that led him to shun to declare the whole truth for fear of offending, led him to act a falsehood in pointing to the golden calf as a representation of the One who brought them from Egypt. Thus one unfaithfulness leads to another (Letter 10, 1896).

4, 5 Idol Proclaimed God.—The result of their murmuring and unbelief was that Aaron made them a golden calf to represent God. He proclaimed this idol to be God, and a great deal of enthusiasm was created over this false God (The Review and Herald, September 6, 1906).

19 Tables of Law Purposely Broken.—In utter discouragement and wrath because of their great sin, he [Moses] threw down the tables of stone by divine direction purposely to break them in the sight of the people, and thus signify that they had broken the covenant so recently made with God (The Signs of the Times, May 20, 1880).

Chapter 34

28 (Matthew 4:1-11). No Pangs of Hunger.—Moses had, on special occasions, been thus long [forty days] without food. But he felt not the pangs of hunger. He was not harassed and tormented by a vile yet powerful foe. Moses was elevated above the human, and was enshrouded in the glory of God, and was especially sustained of God. The excellent glory inclosed him (Redemption: or the First Advent of Christ, pages 47, 48).

29 Christ Is the Glory of the Law.—The glory that shone on the face of Moses was a reflection of the righteousness of Christ in the law. The law itself would have no glory, only that in it Christ is embodied. It has no power to save. It is lusterless only as in it Christ is represented as full of righteousness and truth (The Review and Herald, April 22, 1902).

29-33 (2 Corinthians 3:13-15). Moses Saw the Day of Christ.—In the mount, when the law was given to Moses, the Coming One was shown to him also. He saw Christ's work, and His mission to earth, when the Son of God should take upon Himself humanity, and become a teacher and a guide to the world, and at last give Himself a ransom for their sins. When the perfect Offering should be made for the sins of men, the sacrificial offerings typifying the work of the Messiah were to cease. With the advent of Christ, the veil of uncertainty was to be lifted, and a flood of light shed upon the darkened understanding of His people.

As Moses saw the day of Christ, and the new and living way of salvation that was to be opened through His blood, he was captivated and entranced. The praise of God was in his heart, and the divine glory that attended the giving of the law was so strikingly revealed in his countenance when he came down from the mount to walk with Israel, that the brightness was painful. Because of their transgressions, the people were unable to look upon his face, and he wore a veil that he might not terrify them....

Had the Israelites discerned the gospel light that was opened to Moses, had they been able by faith to look steadfastly to the end of that which was abolished, they could have endured the light which was reflected from the countenance of Moses. "But their minds were blinded; for until this day remaineth the same veil untaken away in the reading of the Old Testament; which veil is done away in Christ." The Jews as a people did not discern that the Messiah whom they rejected, was the Angel who guided their fathers in their travels in the wilderness. To this day the veil is upon their hearts, and its darkness hides from them the good news of salvation through the merits of a crucified Redeemer (The Signs of the Times, August 25, 1887).

Leviticus

Chapter 1

1, 2 Become Familiar With Levitical Law.—We are to become familiar with the Levitical law in all its bearings; for it contains rules that must be obeyed; it contains the instruction that if studied will enable us to understand better the rule of faith and practice that we are to follow in our dealings with one another. No soul has any excuse for being in darkness. Those who receive Christ by faith will receive also power to become the sons of God (Letter 3, 1905).

3 (Malachi 1:13). Every Sacrifice Inspected by God.—It is Christ who searches the hearts and tries the reins of the children of men. All things are naked and open before the eyes of Him with whom we have to do, neither is there any creature that is not manifest in His sight. In the days of ancient Israel the sacrifices brought to the high priest were cut open to the backbone to see if they were sound at heart. So the sacrifices we bring today are laid open before the piercing eye of our great High Priest. He opens and inspects every sacrifice brought by the human race, that He may prove whether it is worthy of being presented to the Father (MS 42, 1901).

Chapter 5

6 Bring a Trespass Offering.—Let the members of every family begin to work over against their own houses. Let them humble themselves before God. It would be well to have a trespass-offering box in sight, and have all the household agree that whosoever speaks unkindly of another or utters angry words, shall drop into the trespass-offering box a certain sum of money. This would put them upon their guard against the wicked words which work injury, not only to their brethren, but to themselves. No man of himself can tame the unruly member, the tongue; but God will do the work for him who comes unto Him with contrite heart in faith and with humble supplication. By the help of God, bridle your tongues; talk less, and pray more (The Review and Herald, March 12, 1895).

Chapter 8

31 Sin Offering of Officiating Priest.—The sins of the people were transferred in figure to the officiating priest, who was a mediator for the people. The priest could not himself become an offering for sin, and make an atonement with his life, for he was also a sinner. Therefore, instead of suffering death himself, he killed a lamb without blemish; the penalty of sin was transferred to the innocent beast, which thus became his immediate substitute, and typified the perfect offering of Jesus Christ. Through the blood of this victim, man looked forward by faith to the blood of Christ which would atone for the sins of the world (The Signs of the Times, March 14, 1878).

Chapter 10

1 (Ch. 16:12, 13) Strange Fire Offered Today.—God has not changed. He is as particular and exact in His requirements now as He was in the days of Moses. But in the sanctuaries of worship in our day, with the songs of praise, the prayers, and the teaching from the pulpit, there is not merely strange fire, but positive defilement. Instead of truths being preached with holy unction from God, it is sometimes spoken under the influence of tobacco and brandy. Strange fire indeed! Bible truth and Bible holiness are presented to the people, and prayers are offered to God, mingled with the stench of tobacco! Such incense is most acceptable to Satan! A terrible deception is this! What an offence in the sight of God! What an insult to Him who is holy, dwelling in light unapproachable!

If the faculties of the mind were in healthful vigor, professed Christians would discern the inconsistency of such worship. Like Nadab and Abihu, their sensibilities are so blunted that they make no difference between the sacred and common. Holy and sacred things are brought down upon a level with their tobacconized breaths, benumbed brains, and their polluted souls, defiled through indulgence of appetite and passion. Professed Christians eat and drink, smoke and chew tobacco, and become gluttons and drunkards, to gratify appetite, and still talk of overcoming as Christ overcame! (The Review and Herald, March 25, 1875).

Chapter 14

4-8 (John 1:29). Two Birds—One Dipped in Blood.—The wonderful symbol of the living bird dipped in the blood of the bird slain and then set free to its joyous life, is to us the symbol of the atonement. There were death and life blended, presenting to the searcher for truth the hidden treasure, the union of the pardoning blood with the resurrection and life of our Redeemer. The bird slain was over living water; that flowing stream was a symbol of the ever flowing, ever cleansing efficacy of the blood of Christ, the Lamb slain from the foundation of the world, the fountain that was open for Judah and Jerusalem, wherein they may wash and be clean from every stain of sin. We are to have free access to the atoning blood of Christ. This we must regard as the most precious privilege, the greatest blessing, ever granted to sinful man. And how little is made of this great gift! How deep, how wide and continuous is this stream! To every soul thirsting after holiness there is repose, there is rest, there is the quickening influence of the Holy Spirit, and then the holy, happy, peaceful walk and precious communion with Christ. Then, oh, then, can we intelligently say with John, "Behold the Lamb of God, that taketh away the sin of the world" (Letter 87, 1894).

Chapter 16

23, 24 Garments of the High Priest.—As the high priest laid aside his pontifical dress, and officiated in the white linen dress of a common priest, so Christ emptied Himself, and took the form of a servant, and offered sacrifice, Himself the priest, Himself the victim. As the high priest, after performing his service in the holy of holies, came forth to the waiting congregation in his pontifical robes, so Christ will come the second time clothed in glorious garments of the whitest white, "such as no fuller on earth can whiten them." He will come in His own glory, and in the glory of His Father, as King of kings and Lord of lords, and all the angelic host will escort Him on His way (MS 113, 1899).

Chapter 17

11 (Matthew 26:28; Hebrews 9:22). Blood Was Sacred.—The blood of the Son of God was symbolized by the blood of the slain victim, and God would have clear and definite ideas preserved between the sacred and the common. Blood was sacred, inasmuch as through the shedding of the blood of the Son of God alone could there be atonement for sin (The Signs of the Times, July 15, 1880).

Chapter 25

10 Year of Jubilee.—Every fiftieth year, the year of jubilee, every inheritance in the land was to be restored to its original owner. "In the year of jubilee ye shall return every man unto his possession," God declared.

Thus in His infinite wisdom the Lord educated His people. His requirements were not arbitrary. Connected with all the instruction received by the people from the Source of all light was the consequence of obedience and disobedience. They were taught that obedience would bring them the richest spiritual grace, and would enable them to distinguish between the sacred and the common. Disobedience would also bring its sure result. If the people chose to manage the land in their own supposed wisdom, they would find that the Lord would not work a miracle to counteract the evils He was trying to save them from.

The Lord presented to His people the course they must pursue if they would be a prosperous, independent nation. If they obeyed Him, He declared that health and peace would be theirs, and under His supervision the land would yield its increase (MS 121, 1899).

18-22 Agricultural and Tithing Laws a Test.—The tithing system was instituted by the Lord as the very best arrangement to help the people in carrying out the principles of the law. If this law were obeyed, the people would be entrusted with the entire vineyard, the whole earth. [Quotes Leviticus 25:18-22.] ...

Men were to cooperate with God in restoring the diseased land to health, that it might be a praise and a glory to His name. And as the land they possessed would, if managed with skill and earnestness, produce its treasures, so their hearts, if controlled by God, would reflect His character....

In the laws which God gave for the cultivation of the soil, He was giving the people opportunity to overcome their selfishness and become heavenly-minded. Canaan would be to them as Eden if they obeyed the Word of the Lord. Through them the Lord designed to teach all the nations of the world how to cultivate the soil so that it would yield healthy fruit, free from disease. The earth is the Lord's vineyard, and is to be treated according to His plan. Those who cultivated the soil were to realize that they were doing God service. They were as truly in their lot and place as were the men appointed to minister in the priesthood and in work connected with the tabernacle. God told the people that the Levites were a gift to them, and no matter what their trade, they were to help to support them (Ibid.).

Numbers

Chapter 11

4 Diet Modified Disposition, Activated Mind.—The state of the mind has largely to do with the health of the body, and especially with the health of the digestive organs. As a general thing, the Lord did not provide His people with flesh meat in the desert, because He knew that the use of this diet would create disease and insubordination. In order to modify the disposition, and bring the higher powers of the mind into active exercise, He removed from them the flesh of dead animals. He gave them angel's food, manna from heaven (MS 38, 1898).

Chapter 12

1 Moses' Wife Not Black.—The wife of Moses was not black, but her complexion was somewhat darker than the Hebrews (The Spirit of Prophecy 1:286).

3 Moses Superior to All Rulers.—Moses stands forth superior in wisdom and integrity to all the sovereigns and statesmen of earth. Yet this man claims no credit for himself, but points the people to God as the Source of all power and wisdom. Where is there such a character among men of this age? Those who would speak contemptuously of the law of God are dishonoring Him and casting a shadow over the most illustrious character presented in the annals of men (The Signs of the Times, October 21, 1886).

(Exodus 18:13). Moses Could Judge Instantly.—Moses was a humble man; God called him the meekest man on earth. He was generous, noble, well-balanced; he was not defective, and his qualities were not merely half developed. He could successfully exhort his fellow-men, because his life itself was a living representation of what man can become and accomplish with God as his helper, of what he taught to others, of what he desired them to be, and of what God required of him. He spoke from the heart and it reached the heart. He was accomplished in knowledge and yet simple as a child in the manifestation of his deep sympathies. Endowed with a remarkable instinct, he could judge instantly of the needs of all who surrounded him, and of the things which were in bad condition and required attention, and he did not neglect them (MS 24, 1887).

The Meekest of Men.—Moses was the greatest man who ever stood as leader of the people of God. He was greatly honored by God, not for the experience which he had gained in the Egyptian court, but because he was the meekest of men. God talked with him face to face, as a man talks with a friend. If men desire to be honored by God, let them be humble. Those who carry forward God's work should be distinguished from all others by their humility. Of the man who is noted for his meekness, Christ says, He can be trusted. Through him I can reveal Myself to the world. He will not weave into the web any threads of selfishness. I will manifest Myself to him as I do not to the world (MS 165, 1899).

Chapter 13

30 Courage Through Faith.—It was Caleb's faith that gave him courage, that kept him from the fear of man, and enabled him to stand boldly and unflinchingly in the defense of the right. Through reliance on the same Power, the mighty General of the armies of heaven, every true soldier of the cross may receive strength and courage to overcome the obstacles that seem insurmountable (The Review and Herald, May 30, 1912).

(Zechariah 4:6). Calebs Needed Today.—Calebs have been greatly needed in different periods of the history of our work. Today we need men of thorough fidelity, men who follow the Lord fully, men who are not disposed to be silent when they ought to speak, who are as true as steel to principle, who do not seek to make a pretentious show, but who walk humbly with God, patient, kind, obliging, courteous men, who understand that the science of prayer is to exercise faith and show works that will tell to the glory of God and the good of His people.... To follow Jesus requires wholehearted conversion at the start, and a repetition of this conversion every day (Letter 39, 1899).

Chapter 14

29, 30 (Ch. 26:64, 65). Wanderings Extended Through Satan's Efforts.— God gave positive evidence that He rules in the heavens, and rebellion was punished with death. Only two of those who as adults left Egypt, saw the promised land. The wanderings of the people were extended until the rest were buried in the wilderness.

Today Satan is using the same devising to introduce the same evils, and his efforts are followed by the same results that in the days of Israel laid so many in their graves (MS 13, 1906).

Chapter 15

38, 39 (1 Timothy 2:9, 10; 1 Peter 3:3, 4). Israel's Dress Distinguished Them From Nations.— The children of Israel, after they were brought out of Egypt, were commanded to have a simple ribbon of blue in the border of their garments, to distinguish them from the nations around them, and to signify that they were God's peculiar people. The people of God are not now required to have a special mark placed upon their garments. But in the New Testament we are often referred to ancient Israel for examples. If God gave such definite directions to His ancient people in regard to their dress, will not the dress of His people in this age come under His notice? Should there not be in their dress a distinction from that of the world? Should not the people of God, who are His peculiar treasure, seek even in their dress to glorify God? And should they not be examples in point of dress, and by their simple style rebuke the pride, vanity, and extravagance of worldly, pleasure-loving professors? God requires this of His people. Pride is rebuked in His Word (The Health Reformer, February 1872).

Chapter 16

1-50 Rebellion Against Leadership.—These men of Israel complained, and influenced the people to stand with them in rebellion, and even after God stretched forth His hand and swallowed up the wrong-doers, and the people fled to their tents in horror, their rebellion was not cured. The depth of their disaffection was made manifest even under the judgment of the Lord. The morning after the destruction of Korah, Dathan, and Abiram and their confederates, the people came to Moses and Aaron, saying, "Ye have killed the people of the Lord." For this false charge on the servants of God, thousands more were killed, for there was in them sin, exultation and presumptuous wickedness (Letter 12a, 1893).

(1 Samuel 15:23). Lessons From the Rebellion.—I question whether genuine rebellion is ever curable. Study in Patriarchs and Prophets the rebellion of Korah, Dathan, and Abiram. This rebellion was extended, including more than two men. [Reference is here made to two men leading a rebellion in a certain field.—Editor.] It was led by two hundred and fifty princes of the congregation, men of renown. Call rebellion by its right name, and apostasy by its right name, and then consider that the experience of the ancient people of God with all its objectionable features was faithfully chronicled to pass into history. The Scripture declares, "These things were written for our admonition, upon whom the ends of the world are come." And if men and women who have the knowledge of the truth are so far separated from their great Leader, that they will take the great leader of apostasy, and name him Christ our

Righteousness, it is because they have not sunk the shaft deep into the mines of truth. They are not able to distinguish the precious ore from the base material....

The Lord has permitted this matter to develop as it has done, in order to show how easily His people will be misled, when they depend upon the words of men instead of searching the Scriptures for themselves, as did the noble Bereans, to see if these things are so....

Rebellion and apostasy are in the very air we breathe. We shall be affected by it unless we by faith hang our helpless souls upon Christ. If men are so easily misled, how will they stand when Satan shall personate Christ, and work miracles? Who will be unmoved by his misrepresentations? Professing to be Christ when it is only Satan assuming the person of Christ, and apparently working the works of Christ? What will hold God's people from giving their allegiance to false Christs? "Go not ye after them."

The doctrines must be plainly understood. The men accepted to teach the truth must be anchored; then their vessel will hold against storm and tempest, because the anchor holds them firmly. The deceptions will increase, and we are to call rebellion by its right name. We are to stand with the whole armor on. My brethren, you are not meeting men only, but principalities and powers. We wrestle not against flesh and blood. Let Ephesians 6:10-18 be read carefully (Letter 1, 1897).

Christ came to our world not to aid Satan in working up rebellion, but to put down rebellion. Wherever men start out in rebellion they will work secretly and in darkness, as they will not come as Christ has told them to do to the ones they have any matter against but will take their budget of falsehoods and enmity and evil surmisings and Satanic representations, as did Satan to the fellow angels under him, and gain their sympathy by false representations (Letter 156, 1897).

1-3 Princes Enlisted in Rebellion.—Those men of Israel were determined to resist all evidence that would prove them to be wrong, and they went on and on in their course of disaffection until many were drawn away to unite with them. Who were these? Not the weak, not the ignorant, not the unenlightened. In that rebellion there were two hundred and fifty princes famous in the congregation, men of renown (Letter 2a, 1892).

3 Moses Accused of Hindering Progress.—They accused Moses of being the cause of their not entering the promised land. They said that God had not dealt with them thus. He had not said that they should die in the wilderness. They would never believe that He had thus said; but that it was Moses who had said this, not the Lord; and that it was all arranged by Moses to never bring them to the land of Canaan (Spiritual Gifts 4a:30).

Korah Deceived Himself.—Korah had cherished his envy and rebellion until he was self-deceived, and he really thought that the congregation was a very righteous people, and that Moses was a tyrannical ruler, continually dwelling upon the necessity of the congregation's being holy, when there was no need of it, for they were holy (Spiritual Gifts 4a:31).

19 The People Deceived Themselves.—The people thought if Korah could lead them, and encourage them, and dwell upon their righteous acts, instead of reminding them of their failures, they should have a very peaceful, prosperous journey, and he would without doubt lead them, not back and forward in the wilderness, but into the promised land. They said that it was Moses who had told them that they could not go into the land, and that the Lord had not thus said. Korah in his exalted self-confidence gathered all the congregation against Moses and Aaron, "unto the door of the tabernacle of the congregation" (Ibid.).

Chapter 17

1-13 Rod Preserved as Reminder.—All the remarkable changes in the rod occurred in one night, to convince them that God had positively distinguished between Aaron and the rest of the children of Israel. After this miracle of divine power, the authority of the priesthood was no longer called in question. This wonderful rod was preserved to be frequently shown to the people to remind them of the past, to prevent them from murmuring, and again calling in question to whom the priesthood rightfully belonged. After the children of Israel were fully convinced of their wrong, in unjustly accusing Moses and

Aaron, as they had done, they saw their past rebellion in its true light, and they were terrified. They spake unto Moses, saying, "Behold we die, we perish; we all perish." They are at length compelled to believe the unwelcome truth, that their fate is to die in the wilderness. After they believed that it was indeed the Lord who had said they should not enter the promised land, but should die, they then acknowledged that Moses and Aaron were right, and that they had sinned against the Lord, in rebelling against their authority. They also confessed that Korah, and those who perished with him, were sinners against the Lord and that they had justly suffered His wrath (Spiritual Gifts 4a:35, 36).

Chapter 20

7, 8, 10, 12 Sin of Moses Misrepresented God's Leadership.—In all their wanderings, the children of Israel were tempted to attribute to Moses the special work of God, the mighty miracles that had been wrought to deliver them from Egyptian bondage. They charged Moses with bringing them out of the land of Egypt. It was true that God had manifested Himself wonderfully to Moses. He had specially favored him with His presence. To him God had revealed His exceeding glory. Upon the mount He had taken him into a sacred nearness to Himself, and had talked with him as a man speaks to a friend. But the Lord had given evidence after evidence that it was He Himself who was working for their deliverance.

By saying, "Must we fetch you water out of this rock?" Moses virtually said to the people that they were correct in believing that he himself was doing the mighty works that had been done in their behalf. This made it necessary for God to prove to Israel that his admission was not founded on fact.... To dispel forever from the minds of the Israelites the idea that a man was leading them, God found it necessary to allow their leader to die before they entered the land of Canaan (MS 69, 1912).

Chapter 21

6 Had Been Miraculously Preserved.—To punish them for their ingratitude, and complaining against God, the Lord permitted fiery serpents to bite them. They were called fiery, because their bite produced painful inflammation, and speedy death. The Israelites, up to this time, had been preserved from these serpents in the wilderness, by a continual miracle; for the wilderness through which they traveled was infested with poisonous serpents (Spiritual Gifts 4a:41).

A Fatal Decision.—There were those who stopped to reason regarding the foolishness of looking for relief to this means. That they should be healed by looking at a piece of brass was absurd to their minds, and they said, "We will not look." This decision was fatal, and all who would not accept the provision made perished.

The brazen serpent was uplifted in the wilderness that those who looked in faith might be made whole. In like manner God sends a restoring, healing message to men, calling upon them to look away from man and earthly things, and place their trust in God. He has given His people the truth with power through the Holy Spirit. He opened His Word to those who were searching and praying for truth. But when these messengers gave the truth they had received to the people, they were as unbelieving as the Israelites. Many are cavilling over the truth brought to them by humble messengers (MS 75, 1899).

Chapter 22

1-6 Balaam, Double-Minded.—At the time Balak sent messengers for him [Balaam], he was double-minded, pursuing a course to gain and retain the favor and honor of the enemies of the Lord, for the sake of rewards he received from them. At the same time he was professing to be a prophet of God. Idolatrous nations believed that curses might be uttered which would affect individuals, and even whole nations (Spiritual Gifts 4a:43).

15-17 Balaam's One Sin, Covetousness.—Here is a solemn warning for the people of God today, to allow no unchristian trait to live in their hearts. A sin which is fostered becomes habitual; and, strengthened by repetition, it soon exerts a controlling influence, bringing into subjection all the nobler powers. Balaam loved the reward of unrighteousness. The sin of covetousness, which God ranks with idolatry, he did not resist and overcome. Satan obtained entire control of him through this one fault, which deteriorated his character, and made him a time-server. He called God his master; but he did not serve Him; he did not work the works of God (The Signs of the Times, November 18, 1880).

Chapter 24

1-5 Beheld Glory of God's Presence.—Balaam had wished to appear to be favorable to Balak, and had permitted him to be deceived, and think that he used superstitious ceremonies and enchantments when he besought the Lord. But as he followed out the command given him of God, he grew bolder in proportion as he obeyed the divine impulse, and he laid aside his pretended conjuration, and, looking toward the encampment of the Israelites, he beholds them all encamped in perfect order, under their respective standards, at a distance from the tabernacle. Balaam was permitted to behold the glorious manifestation of God's presence, overshadowing protecting, and guiding the tabernacle. He was filled with admiration at the sublime scene. He opened his parable with all the dignity of a true prophet of God (Spiritual Gifts 4a:47, 48).

15-24 Balak Amazed by Revelation.—The Moabites understood the import of the prophetic words of Balaam—that the Israelites after conquering the Canaanites, should settle in their land, and all attempts to subdue them would be of no more avail than for a feeble beast to arouse the lion out of his den. Balaam told Balak that he would inform him what the Israelites should do to his people at a later period. The Lord unfolded the future before Balaam, and permitted events which would occur, to pass before his sight, that the Moabites should understand that Israel should finally triumph. As Balaam prophetically rehearsed the future to Balak and his princes, he was struck with amazement at the future display of God's power (Spiritual Gifts 4a:48).

Chapter 25

16-18 God's Control Unlimited.—Moses commanded the men of war to destroy the women and male children. Balaam had sold the children of Israel for a reward, and he perished with the people whose favor he had obtained at the sacrifice of twenty-four thousand of the Israelites. The Lord is regarded as cruel by many in requiring His people to make war with other nations. They say that it is contrary to His benevolent character. But He who made the world, and formed man to dwell upon the earth, has unlimited control over all the works of His hands, and it is His right to do as He pleases, and what He pleases with the work of His hands. Man has no right to say to his Maker, Why doest Thou thus? There is no injustice in His character. He is the Ruler of the world, and a large portion of His subjects have rebelled against His authority, and have trampled upon His law.... He has used His people as instruments of His wrath, to punish wicked nations, who have vexed them, and seduced them into idolatry (Spiritual Gifts 4a:50, 51).

Chapter 26

64. See EGW comment on Numbers 14:29.

Chapter 29

12-39. See EGW comment on Exodus 23:16.

Deuteronomy

Chapter 1

1 Study Deuteronomy Carefully.—The book of Deuteronomy should be carefully studied by those living on the earth today. It contains a record of the instruction given to Moses to give to the children of Israel. In it the law is repeated....

The law of God was often to be repeated to Israel. That it precepts might not be forgotten, it was to be kept before the people, and was ever to be exalted and honored. Parents were to read the law to their children, teaching it to them line upon line, precept upon precept. And on public occasions the law was to be read in the hearing of all the people.

Upon obedience to this law depended the prosperity of Israel. If they were obedient, it would bring them life; if disobedient, death (The Review and Herald, December 31, 1903).

(Exodus 1:1). Study Deuteronomy and Exodus More.—We do not make enough of Deuteronomy and Exodus. These books record the dealings of God with Israel. God took the Israelites from slavery, and led them through the wilderness to the promised land (MS 11, 1903).

6-10. Israel's Invisible Leader Ruled Through Visible Agents.—The Lord God of heaven is our Leader. He is a leader whom we can safely follow; for He never makes a mistake. Let us honor God and His Son Jesus Christ, through whom He communicates with the world. It was Christ who gave to Moses the instruction that He gave to the children of Israel. It was Christ who delivered the Israelites from Egyptian bondage. Moses and Aaron were the visible leaders of the people. To Moses instruction was given by their invisible Leader, to be repeated to them.

Had Israel obeyed the directions given them by Moses, not one of those who started on the journey from Egypt would in the wilderness have fallen a prey to disease or death. They were under a safe Guide. Christ had pledged Himself to lead them safely to the promised land if they would follow His guidance. This vast multitude, numbering more than a million people, was under His direct rule. They were His family. In every one of them He was interested (MS 144, 1903).

Chapter 4

1 Study Chapters Four to Eight.—I ask you to study the fourth to the eighth chapters of Deuteronomy, that you may understand what God required of His ancient people that they might be a holy people unto Himself. We are nearing the day of God's great final review, when the people of this world must stand before the Judge of all the earth to answer for their deeds. We are now in the time of investigation. Before the day of God's review, every character will have been investigated, every case decided for eternity. Let the words of God's servant recorded in these chapters be read with profit (Letter 112, 1909).

Chapter 6

1, 2 (quoted). Results of Obedience.—In this scripture we are taught that obedience to God's requirements brings the obedient under the laws that control the physical being. Those who would preserve themselves in health must bring into subjection all appetites and passions. They must not indulge lustful passion and intemperate appetite, for they are to remain under control to God, and their physical, mental, and moral powers are to be so wisely employed that the bodily mechanism will remain in good working order. Health, life, and happiness are the result of obedience to physical laws governing our bodies. If our will and way are in accordance with God's will and way; if we do the pleasure of our Creator, He will keep the human organism in good condition, and restore the moral, mental, and physical powers, in order that He may work through us to His glory. Constantly His restoring power is manifested in our bodies. If we cooperate with Him in this work, health and happiness, peace and usefulness, are the sure results (MS 151, 1901).

6-9 (quoted) (Verse 25; Romans 10:5). Obedience by Faith Is Righteousness by Faith.—When we bring our lives to complete obedience to the law of God, regarding God as our supreme Guide, and clinging to Christ as our hope of righteousness, God will work in our behalf. This is a righteousness of faith, a righteousness hidden in a mystery of which the worldling knows nothing, and which he cannot understand. Sophistry and strife follow in the train of the serpent; but the commandments of God diligently studied and practiced, open to us communication with heaven, and distinguish for us the true from the false. This obedience works out for us the divine will, bringing into our lives the righteousness and perfection that was seen in the life of Christ (MS 43, 1907).

Chapter 9

9. See EGW comment on Exodus 34:28.

Chapter 15

11 No Thread of Selfishness in Web of Life.—Deuteronomy contains much instruction regarding what the law is to us, and the relation we shall sustain to God as we reverence and obey His law.

We are God's servants, doing His service. Into the great web of life we are to draw no thread of selfishness; for this would spoil the pattern. But, oh, how thoughtless men are apt to be! How seldom do they make the interests of God's suffering ones their own. The poor are all around them, but they pass on, thoughtless and indifferent, regardless of the widows and orphans who, left without resources, suffer, but do not tell their need. If the rich would place a small fund in the bank, at the disposal of the needy ones, how much suffering would be saved. The holy love of God should lead every one to see that it is his duty to care for some other one, and thus keep alive the spirit of benevolence.... With what goodness, mercy, and love God lays His requirements before His children, telling them what they are to do. He honors us by making us His helping hand. Instead of complaining, let us rejoice that we have the privilege of serving under so good and merciful a Master (Letter 112, 1902).

Chapter 18

10 (Leviticus 18:21; 20:2, 3). Trial by Fire Condemned.—God was a wise and compassionate Lawgiver, judging all cases righteously, and without partiality. While the Israelites were in Egyptian bondage, they were surrounded by idolatry. The Egyptians had received traditions in regard to sacrificing. They did not acknowledge the existence of the God of heaven. They sacrificed to their idol gods. With great pomp and ceremony they performed their idol worship. They erected altars to the honor of their gods, and they required even their own children to pass through the fire. After they had erected their altars, they required their children to leap over the altars through the fire. If they could do this without their being burned, the idol priests and people received it as an evidence that their God accepted their offerings, and favored especially the person who passed through the fiery ordeal. He was loaded with benefits, and was ever afterward greatly esteemed by all the people. He was never allowed to be punished, however aggravating might be his crimes. If another person who leaped through the fire was so unfortunate as to be burned, then his fate was fixed; for they thought that their gods were angry, and would be appeased with nothing short of the unhappy victim's life, and he was offered up as a sacrifice upon their idol altars.

Even some of the children of Israel had so far degraded themselves as to practice these abominations, and God caused the fire to kindle upon their children, whom they made to pass through the fire. They did not go to all the lengths of the heathen nations; but God deprived them of their children by causing the fire to consume them in the act of passing through it.

Because the people of God had confused ideas of the ceremonial sacrificial offerings, and had heathen traditions confounded with their ceremonial worship, God condescended to give them definite directions, that they might understand the true import of those sacrifices which were to last only till the Lamb of God should be slain, who was the great antitype of all their sacrificial offerings (Spiritual Gifts 3:303, 304).

Chapter 23

14 No Uncleanness of Body, Word, or Spirit.—In order to be acceptable in God's sight, the leaders of the people were to give strict heed to the sanitary condition of the armies of Israel, even when they went forth to battle. Every soul, from the commander-in-chief to the lowest soldier in the army, was sacredly charged to preserve cleanliness in his person and surroundings; for the Israelites were chosen by God as His peculiar people. They were sacredly bound to be holy in body and spirit. They were not to be careless or neglectful of their personal duties. In every respect they were to preserve cleanliness. They were to allow nothing untidy or unwholesome in their surroundings, nothing which would taint the purity of the atmosphere. Inwardly and outwardly they were to be pure [Deuteronomy 23:14 quoted] (Letter 35, 1901).

We know His will, and any departure from it to follow ideas of your own is a dishonor to His name, a reproach to His sacred truth. Everything that relates to the worship of God on earth, is to bear in appearance a striking resemblance to heavenly things. There must be no careless disregard in these things, if you expect the Lord to favor you with His presence. He will not have His work placed on a level with common, temporal things (MS 7, 1889).

All those who come into His presence should give special attention to the body and the clothing. Heaven is a clean and holy place. God is pure and holy. All who come into His presence should take heed to His directions, and have the body and the clothing in a pure, clean condition, thus showing respect to themselves and to Him. The heart must also be sanctified. Those who do this will not dishonor His sacred name by worshiping Him while their hearts are polluted and their apparel is untidy. God sees these things. He marks the heart-preparation, the thoughts, the cleanliness in appearance, of those who worship Him (MS 126 1901).

Chapter 26

8 Wonders Showed God's Power.—The Lord brought up His people from their long servitude in a signal manner, giving the Egyptians an opportunity to exhibit the feeble wisdom of their mighty men, and array the power of their gods in opposition to the God of heaven. The Lord showed them by His servant Moses that the Maker of the heavens and the earth is the living and all-powerful God, above all gods. That His strength was mightier than the strongest—that OMNIPOTENCE could bring forth His people with a high hand and with an outstretched arm. The signs and miracles performed in the presence of Pharaoh were not given for his benefit alone, but for the advantage of God's people, to give them more clear and exalted views of God, and that all Israel should fear Him, and be willing and anxious to leave Egypt, and choose the service of the true and merciful God. Had it not been for these wonderful manifestations, many would have been satisfied to remain in Egypt rather than to journey through the wilderness (Spiritual Gifts 3:204, 205).

16 Withhold Nothing.—There must be no withholding on our part, of our service or our means, if we would fulfill our covenant with God [Deuteronomy 26:16 quoted]. The purpose of all God's commandments is to reveal man's duty not only to God, but to his fellow man. In this late age of the world's history, we are not, because of the selfishness of our hearts, to question or dispute the right of God to make these requirements, or we will deceive ourselves, and rob our souls of the richest blessings of the grace of God. Heart and mind and soul are to be merged in the will of God. Then the covenant, framed from the dictates of infinite wisdom, and made binding by the power and authority of the King of kings and Lord of lords, will be our pleasure. God will have no controversy with us in regard to these binding precepts. It is enough that He has said that obedience to His statutes and laws is the life and prosperity of His people (MS 67, 1907).

18 (Romans 6:3, 4). Mutual Pledge and Mutual Blessing.—The blessings of God's covenant are mutual [Deuteronomy 26:18 quoted]. ...

By our baptismal pledge we avouched and solemnly confessed the Lord Jehovah as our Ruler. We virtually took a solemn oath, in the name of the Father, and of the Son, and of the Holy Ghost, that henceforth our lives would be merged into the life of these three great Agencies, that the life we should live in the flesh would be lived in faithful obedience to God's sacred law. We declared ourselves dead, and our life hid with Christ in God, that henceforth we should walk with Him in newness of life, as men and women having experienced the new birth. We acknowledged God's covenant with us, and pledged ourselves to seek those things which are above, where Christ sitteth on the right hand of God. By our profession of faith we acknowledged the Lord as our God, and yielded ourselves to obey His commandments. By obedience to God's Word we testify before angels and men that we live by every word that proceedeth out of the mouth of God (Ibid.).

Chapter 30

15-19 (Joshua 24:15). Decision to Be Based on Evidence.—It is not the plan of God to compel men to yield their wicked unbelief. Before them are light and darkness, truth and error. It is for them to decide which to accept. The human mind is endowed with power to discriminate between right and wrong. God designs that men shall not decide from impulse, but from weight of evidence, carefully comparing scripture with scripture (Redemption: or the Miracles of Christ, pp. 112, 113).

Other books that we publish in this same size (A4):

1. The Two Babylons, Author: Alexander Hislop.
2. The War of the Jwes, Author: Flavius Josephus.
3. The Secret Terrorists, Author: Bill Hughes.
4. Final Time Events, Author: Ellen G. White.
5. Lessons from the Life of Daniel, Author: Ellen G. White. (6*9)
6. The Book of the Martyrs of Jesus, Author: John Foxe.
7. Healthful Living, Author: Ellen White
8. Receive The Holy Spirit, Author: Alonzo T. Jones.
9. Youth's Instructor Periodical Articles 2 Volumes, Author: Ellen G. White.
10. The Great Controversy Study Guide 2023 edition, Author: D. E. Robinson.
11. Christian Temperance and Bible Hygiene, Author: Ellen G. White.
12. Lessons from the Life of Solomon, Author: Ellen G. White. (6*9)
13. Lessons from the Life of Nehemiah with study guide, Ellen White.
14. 1888 Materials; Volumes 1-4, Author: Ellen G. White.
15. The Law and The Gospel, Author: Ellet J. Waggoner.
16. The Third Angels Message; 3 Volumes, Author: A. T. Jones.
17. The Conflict of the Ages Series in this size(A4), Author: Ellen G. White.
18. Ministry of Healing in this size(A4), Author: Ellen G. White.

* If you wish to purchase them wholesale (40% discount), they are in boxes of 50 books (can be mixed) and you can contact us at this e-mail address: lsdistribution07@gmail.com

www.ingramcontent.com/pod-product-compliance
Lightning Source LLC
LaVergne TN
LVHW062047070526
838201LV00080B/2153